MOTHERWELL FC
Miscellany

MOTHERWELL FC
Miscellany

Steelmen Trivia,
History, Facts & Stats

DEREK WILSON

MOTHERWELL FC
Miscellany

All statistics, facts and figures are correct as of 5th May 2009

© Derek Wilson

Derek Wilson has asserted his rights in accordance with the Copyright,
Designs and Patents Act 1988 to be identified as the author of this work.

Published By:
Pitch Publishing (Brighton) Ltd
A2 Yeoman Gate
Yeoman Way
Durrington
BN13 3QZ

Email: info@pitchpublishing.co.uk
Web: www.pitchpublishing.co.uk

First published 2009

A catalogue record for this book is available from the British Library.

10-digit ISBN: 1-9054114-4-8
13-digit ISBN: 978-1-9054114-4-3

Printed and bound in Malta by Gutenburg Press

For Anne, who kept me going.

FOREWORD BY STEPHEN CRAIGAN

I must be honest in that when I arrived at Motherwell on September 22nd 1994 I knew very little about the football club, its history, or what it meant to be a 'Well fan.

Years on – and with the majority of my adult life spent plying my trade at Fir Park – pride, commitment and dedication is something that I've realised we all have in common at Motherwell FC. "Always expect the unexpected" is a frequently used phrase and as a supporter that's what makes the life of a Motherwell fan exciting, if also frustrating, at times!

In my time at Fir Park I have been honoured to serve as a player, captain and, if only for a few days, manager. Who can forget the scenes at Easter Road when we reached the CIS Cup Final in 2005, the sight of 18,000 Motherwell fans at Hampden for the final, and the magnificent achievement of securing third place in the SPL in 2007/08? European football followed, if only briefly, but the scenes that greeted the players in Nancy sent shivers down my spine and made me proud to be leading my club into Europe.

Like all football clubs, there have been many players and managers who have come and gone over time but the foundation of our club and its supporters will remain. The highs undoubtedly supplement the lows, but over the years the players and, perhaps even more so, the fans have always shown tremendous resilience in the face of adversity. It is that which makes the club special and fills me full of pride to be part of its history. Let's hope this continues and everyone involved with Motherwell FC will be rewarded with success in the years to come.

Stephen Craigan,
Motherwell captain

INTRODUCTION

The *Motherwell Miscellany* is a collection of the statistics, tales and anecdotes behind the history of this great club. There have been many highs and lows from the formation of the club in 1886 all the way through to successive European campaigns in contemporary times.

Thankfully, on the path of the club's 123-year history there have been plenty of incidents which we can look back on with fondness. Not all of them were good at the time, of course, but the setbacks can now be viewed in a bittersweet light. After all, each failure brings us one step closer to that elusive success. Doesn't it?!

This book was both a tremendous challenge and a tremendous pleasure to write. The help of other excellent books written by Graham Barnstaple, Keith Brown, John Swinburne, Genge Fry, Jim Jeffrey and Alex Smith were essential while Keith Brown, John Swinburne and Alan Burrows, of Motherwell FC, were also a tremendous assistance. I wish you the same enjoyment in reading the book as I had in writing it.

Derek Wilson

ACKNOWLEDGEMENTS

This project required reference to several other excellent books on Motherwell which had been previously written. *A History of the Steelmen* by John Swinburne, *The Men who made Motherwell* by Jim Jeffrey and Genge Fry, *'Well Again* by Graham Barnstaple and Keith Brown and *Motherwell Champions of Scotland* were all invaluable, as was the news archive on James Reid's website, www.motherwellfc.org.

Once more, the Motherwell Heritage Centre and its collection of *Motherwell Times* newspapers was also crucial. My father John was a dedicated assistant again and both my parents offered hours of support in the form of tea, coffee and curry along with their considerable proofreading skills. Any mistakes in the text are entirely my responsibility. The help of Keith Brown in providing the Motherwell minute books was invaluable and Alan Burrows of Motherwell FC was tremendously helpful during a busy time for the club.

Thanks are also due to Dan Tester at Pitch Publishing for giving me the chance to write this book and also for being very understanding with the time pressure I was under – which also resulted in him dealing with additional pressure as a result.

Finally, Anne Muras for putting up with me and my moods while working for another year since the last book came out!

DERBY KINGS

Motherwell's status as the pride of Lanarkshire is backed up by statistics in derby matches. Against the old Airdrieonians, Motherwell won 70 of 163 meetings – with 30 being drawn – while the side have won one and lost one against Airdrie's latest incarnation. Motherwell have won 63 games against Hamilton Academical from 122 meetings, with 25 draws, while lowly Albion Rovers have never actually managed a win against the Steelmen. They did draw seven games but suffered 27 losses against the 'shire's top team.

OPENING DAY BLUES

While the fans may always look forward to the start of a new season, the team seem less likely to anticipate it with pleasure. From 1999/00 to 2008/09 the team only managed to win one of ten opening day fixtures – at Love Street in 2007 – while Hearts, Rangers, Celtic (twice), Dundee (twice), Livingston, Dunfermline Athletic and Hibernian all escaped their tussle with the 'Well with at least one point to show for their efforts.

WITH RECKLESS ABANDON

The opposition may conspire against the team on occasion but the weather is also a worthy adversary; twice in recent years Motherwell have been leading at half-time only for the game to be abandoned! In 1999, Hearts succeeded in claiming the pitch was saturated when trailing 1-0 at Fir Park in the league and later in that same season a cup tie at Arbroath was abandoned, with 'Well 1-0 up, due to high winds coming off the North Sea. Shaun Teale and Derek Townsley were the unfortunate players who had their goals purged from the record books but Motherwell did defeat Hearts in the replayed game while a mammoth cup series with Arbroath finally ended with the Steelmen progressing.

THE JOY OF SIX

In the 1953/54 season Motherwell and Dumbarton played out a dramatic 6-6 draw at Fir Park – a record for the highest scoring drawn match in British football. A special thought should go to Archie Williams who scored a hat-trick for the Steelmen but still failed to collect a win bonus!

LEARN FROM YOUR MISTAKES

Andy Paton was awarded the title of greatest-ever Motherwell player at a ceremony in 2007 but even he was not infallible. Early in his career, he was viciously head-butted by an opponent while in the process of shaking hands after a game. At least Andy learned from the experience and from that occasion on, he rarely shook hands with opponents lest the same situation happen again.

HIGH FIVE!

The following players have scored five goals for Motherwell in a competitive game: Hugh Ferguson against Clydebank in 1921 and Galston in 1925; Willie MacFadyen against Third Lanark, in both 1931 and 1932, against Montrose in 1933 and Queen of the South in 1933; Robert Russell against Falkirk in 1962; Bobby Campbell against St. Mirren in 1966. And, the last player to achieve such a feat was Vic Davidson against Alloa Athletic in 1977.

CONSISTENCY BRINGS SUCCESS

In playing ten games to win the Scottish Cup of 1952, Motherwell fielded the same team in nine consecutive matches. Defender Donald McLeod played in the first tie at Forfar Athletic but was replaced by Charlie Cox. The other members of the cup-winning team were Johnston, Kilmarnock, Shaw, Paton, Redpath, Sloan, Humphries, Kelly, Watson and Aitkenhead.

A GENTLEMAN AND A SCHOLAR

One player not commonly mentioned in the list of Motherwell greats – but deserves to be remembered – is Bert McCann. After signing from Queen's Park in 1956, he went on to make over 250 appearances for the club and even became captain. What makes this remarkable is that Bert achieved this, and five Scotland caps, while playing part-time and simultaneously studying for a university degree! Sadly, like the rest of the Ancell Babes team, major honours eluded him although he did appear in three losing Scottish Cup semi-finals.

CUP WINS: 1991

In 1991, Motherwell was a place of contrasts. With local industry being destroyed the future looked bleak for many but the football club was on the way up. The cup run which had started with a sensational win at holders Aberdeen – substitute Steve Kirk scoring the winner after only 14 seconds on the pitch – was a bright beacon for many in the town. An exciting 4-2 win over Falkirk in the fourth round was followed by a dismal display against Morton and only the calm heads of Davie Cooper, Iain Ferguson, Bobby Russell, Steve Kirk and Colin O'Neil in a penalty shoot-out allowed the team to progress to the semi-finals. The original semi-final tie with Celtic finished 0-0 and when Motherwell hit the post late on and had a stonewall penalty denied, there was a feeling of 'here we go again' following previous Hampden disappointments. This group of players was to be different, though, and despite trailing twice in the replay, Celtic were defeated 4-2 thanks to marvellous late goals from O'Neil and Kirk. It ensured a rare 'family final' at Hampden when brothers Tommy and Jim McLean led Motherwell and Dundee United into battle. United were perennial final losers but their experience of the big occasion was advantageous and Motherwell had early let-offs with a goal from Hamish French being disallowed and Freddy van der Hoorn hitting the post. Eventually, the Steelmen settled and though leading 1-0 at the break thanks to a Ferguson header, the true drama was only just beginning. John Clark clattered Ally Maxwell, leaving the 'keeper with severe internal injuries, but the disappointment of losing an equaliser was quickly overcome by goals from Phil O'Donnell and Ian Angus. United refused to give up but despite pulling one back immediately they found their attempts to get into the game foiled. A crack in the defence finally appeared in the last minute when Maxwell, slow off his line due to injury, was beaten to the ball by Darren Jackson. The Arabs must have finally believed their time had come. But, this was Motherwell's year and an extra-time header from Kirk restored the lead. Maxwell, playing on with his horrible injuries, had performed heroically since the clash with Clark but there was one last sensation still to come. In the last minute Malpas looked certain to level with a powerful volley but the 'keeper sprang acrobatically to palm the ball over and win the cup for Motherwell.

COMMERCIALISM GONE MAD

While the Fir Park Board retained some discretion in declining to install advertising hoardings at the ground in the late 1920s, there soon came a point when everything was up for sale. The club had not yet begun to wear advertising on the team strips in 1977 but there was plenty of advertising opportunities with Motherwell, including the chance to sponsor individual games. Barratt Homes were so enthusiastic about their day out at Fir Park after sponsoring the game against Rangers they wanted a helicopter to land on the pitch at half-time. However, the Civil Aviation Authority took a dim view of the stunt and promptly banned it from taking place.

ON SPOT BUT OFF TARGET

Tommy Coyne was a deadly striker for Motherwell in his time at Fir Park but penalty kicks were not always his strong point. Despite being more than willing to step up to the spot, and scoring several, Coyne missed a crucial kick against Dundee United in the cup in 1994 and later that year would have an even more frustrating afternoon. Motherwell were involved in an eight-goal thriller against Falkirk at Fir Park but managed to miss two penalties. Coyne had missed the first one – saved by Tony Parks – but when the team were awarded a second, he was handed the ball again. Once more, Parks made the save from the kick but despite winning his individual battle with the striker, it was not enough. Coyne had the last laugh as his two goals from open play helped the team to a 5-3 win. Dougie Arnott's double, and a long-range strike from Billy Davies provided the other goals.

ON THE SKIVE

The energy crisis of 1972 meant that football clubs were not able to play midweek matches under floodlights and instead had to switch kick-off times to what would normally be viewed as the middle of the working day. One such match was the Scottish Cup replay between Motherwell and Ayr United at Fir Park that the hosts won 2-1. Despite the unusual time of the game, 11,000 fans still turned up to watch – a crowd that would delight the Motherwell Board now, regardless of the circumstances.

GONE BUT NOT FORGOTTEN: DAVIE COOPER

Scottish football was thrown into shock on March 22nd 1995 when Davie Cooper suffered a brain haemorrhage while filming a television series promoting football skills. He died the next day, aged 39. Davie only played at Fir Park from 1989 to 1993 but despite the relatively short length of his Motherwell career, the impact he made on the club was absolutely huge. Arguably, he was the best signing the club made in the modern age. After impressing for Clydebank Cooper was snapped up by Rangers – the team he had supported as a boy – in 1977 and his massive talent was shown on a higher stage. He racked up over 500 appearances for the Ibrox club and collected a host of winners' medals. He was capped by Scotland and scored two crucial goals in 1985 en route to the Mexico World Cup – a penalty against Wales – and then the vital opener against Australia in the two-legged play-off clash. The arrival of Mark Walters at Rangers pushed Cooper out of the side and he moved on to Motherwell, for a mere £50,000, in 1989 in an attempt to extend his career. Cynics may have thought he was just happy to finish his playing days in comfort but they would be proved very wrong. Motherwell had been strugglers in the Premier League since promotion in 1985 but improvements were being made and Cooper was one of the final pieces in the jigsaw. His first season saw the club finish sixth, respectable in itself, but level on points with Celtic, and just a couple short of a European spot that seemed completely unthinkable a few years earlier. The next season Motherwell finished sixth once more but won silverware for the first time in 39 years by collecting the Scottish Cup at Hampden. Many important players had vital roles but the majority of fans believe Cooper was the spark that made a good team great. His impact wasn't restricted to his playing skills as his encouragement and influence did a lot to improve youngsters Tom Boyd and Phil O'Donnell (who were subsequently sold for a total of £2.55m). Davie moved back to his first club, Clydebank, in 1993 and had played in the Scottish Cup just a month before his death. The newly constructed north stand at Fir Park was named in his honour in response to the thousands of fans who flocked to the ground to lay shirts, scarves and flowers following news of his tragic death.

IN SEARCH OF GOALS

Not every Motherwell season is packed with exciting football and plenty of goals. In the 1995/96 campaign, Willie Falconer finished the year as top league scorer for the club despite netting only five times. In fairness to Willie, he was only signed in the second half of the season and his goals were vital in the battle against relegation. However, such a low figure does not say much for the scoring prowess of the rest of the team!

SPLASHING THE CASH

Every so often the club dusted down the cheque book to make a dramatic swoop in the transfer market. Will the club ever spend so much money on a player again?

Player	From	Fee	Year
John Spencer	Everton	£600,000	2000
Mitchell van der Gaag	PSV Eindhoven	£400,000	1995
Shaun McSkimming	Kilmarnock	£350,000	1994
Paul Lambert	St. Mirren	£250,000	1993
John Hendry	Tottenham Hotspur	£200,000	1995

MOVING ON UP

Motherwell have only been relegated four times from the top flight of Scottish football. On three of those occasions the club bounced back to win promotion at the first time of asking; 1953/54, 1968/69 and 1984/85. Relegation in 1978/79 caused the club to miss three campaigns from the highest level before promotion was achieved in 1981/82.

AND NOT GOING DOWN

Much to the annoyance of fans of some other clubs, Motherwell have enjoyed some luck in avoiding relegation. In 1954/55 and 1985/86, league reconstruction saved the side from taking the drop while the abolition of a play-off ensured safety in 1997/98. The team also survived in the SPL in 2002/03 despite finishing bottom due to Falkirk, the side due promotion from the First Division, not having a compliant ground.

PLAYER OF THE YEAR

A Player of the Year award was instigated by the Motherwell Supporters' Association in 1956; Andy Paton took the first honour when Motherwell secretary John Hunter, who had signed him in 1942, presented the player with a silver cup. Famous names such as Ian St. John, Joe Wark and Tommy Coyne have all taken the award but stars such as Willie Pettigrew, Davie Cooper and Dougie Arnott missed out. Charlie Aitken, John Martis, Bobby Watson, Joe Wark, Stuart Rennie, Tom Boyd, Brian Martin and Stephen Craigan won the award twice but no player has been declared Player of the Year on three occasions.

THE YOUNG PRETENDERS

Financial cutbacks mean Motherwell have to throw in players at ever younger ages, resulting in some of the playing staff having already racked up a huge number of appearances. David Clarkson made 250 appearances before turning 24 – on his way to earning a summer transfer to Bristol City – while Stevie Hammell, slightly older at 27, has clocked up 366 appearances in two spells at Fir Park. Hammell, in particular, is well up the post-war list but both are some way short of Joe Wark and Willie Kilmarnock who each played more than 450 games for Motherwell. And, the all-time leader is surely out of sight – Bobby Ferrier played 626 times for the club!

DID YOU KNOW?

In the championship season of 1931/32, Ben Ellis was the only outfield player to appear in every game. Alan Craig and Willie Telfer played in 37 of the 38 league games. Keeper Allan McClory also managed a complete set.

THE 100 PER-CENTERS

Few players have donned the famous claret and amber since the war only to be released despite having a perfect goals-to-games ratio. Despite five strikes in five appearances, William Leitch was released in 1949; and William Sneddon's goal in his only game could not salvage his future at the club in the early 1950s. James Lonie suffered a similar fate as Sneddon a decade later.

MANGLING THE METAPHOR

John Philliben was as high as a kite after an injury-time equaliser at Tannadice in the Scottish Cup of 1994. Sadly for him, the eloquence of his words did not match that of the left-foot with which he struck the dramatic goal, as he spoke of his delight at earning the side "another crack at the cherry". Motherwell lost the replay 1-0 at a packed Fir Park and Dundee United went on to lift the cup by beating Rangers.

WORLD CUP WONDER

Despite producing many international footballers over the years, it took until 1994 before Motherwell were represented at the World Cup. Tommy Coyne played for the Republic of Ireland as they qualified from a tight group with Italy, Norway and Mexico but, unfortunately, lost to Holland in the first knockout round. Davie Cooper would have gone to the Italy World Cup four years previously but pulled out with an injury.

DREAM DEBUT...

It may be the fantasy of every debutant to be introduced as a half-time substitute and win the game with a sensational hat-trick but David Ferrere did just that against Hibs in February 2002. The little Frenchman replaced Scott Leitch at the interval and three fine finishes sent the Motherwell fans into raptures. Another goal by Dirk Lehmann helped complete the 4-0 rout but that was as good as it got for Ferrere. He failed to score again for the team and was one of several players released when the club plunged into administration just a few months later.

...DUD DEBUT

On the other hand, missing a penalty on your debut is a nightmare scenario. Willie Falconer did just that when he failed from the spot at Fir Park against Kilmarnock in January 1996 and a defensive mix-up in the second half allowed the visitors to steal a 1-0 win. However, with the club deep in relegation trouble Falconer quickly put this woe behind him and an excellent spell of form – including five goals – from the big striker helped lead the team to Premier League survival at the expense of Falkirk.

HOME SWEET HOME

Motherwell have used three home grounds since formation in 1886. With speculation frequently linking the club with a move to the brownfield site of Ravenscraig, who knows how long it will be until another location is added to the list?

Roman Road ....Motherwell 3-2 Hamilton, 17th May 1886
Dalziel Park..................Motherwell 3-3 Rangers, 9th March 1889
Fir Park........................... Motherwell 1-8 Celtic, 3rd August 1895

PICTURE PERFECT

Hat-tricks are rare feats for Motherwell players at the best of times but not only did David Clarkson manage one against Dundee United in January 2004, he did it in a 'perfect' fashion. Trailing 1-0 at the break, Clarkson scored a left-footed equaliser from a tight angle before meeting a corner with a firm header to put the hosts into the lead. United pressed but a good finish from the right foot of Clarkson on the break in the dying seconds secured a 3-1 win.

ALMOST PERFECT

Motherwell's championship season of 1931/32 was largely based on the exceptional home form displayed by the side. Out of 19 games played at Fir Park, only Celtic were able to come away with anything while Motherwell triumphed on the other 18 occasions. In total the team scored 72 goals in front of their own fans and conceded only 11 on their way to picking up 37 home points from the 38 available.

LOVE THY NEIGHBOUR

When Motherwell were first relegated in 1953, local rivals Airdrie had a big hand in matters. The Lanarkshire sides had been fighting for survival with several other teams and it was the Diamonds' win over Third Lanark that finally confirmed the Steelmen would drop to the lower league for the first time.

SPOT ON

Motherwell first took part in a penalty shoot-out in the early 1970s when victory was secured against Stoke City in the Texaco Cup. There was a long wait before the next shoot-out which ended in a heartbreaking loss to Celtic in the League Cup semi final of 1986 but thankfully the next contest from 12 yards finished in happier fashion when Morton were dispatched en route to Hampden in the 1991 cup run. Since then, Motherwell were able to successfully see off Clydebank (1995), Inverness (1997) and Raith Rovers (1999) from the spot but suffered losses to Alloa (1996) and Forfar (2003). All of these ties were in the League Cup rather than the Scottish Cup.

FINAL COUNTDOWN

Motherwell's record in major cup finals is as follows:

Year	Tournament	Opponent	Score
1931	Scottish Cup	Celtic	0-1
1933	Scottish Cup	Celtic (after 2-2 draw)	2-4
1939	Scottish Cup	Clyde	0-4
1950	League Cup	Hibernian	3-0
1951	Scottish Cup	Celtic	0-1
1952	Scottish Cup	Dundee	4-0
1954	League Cup	Hearts	2-4
1991	Scottish Cup	Dundee United (AET)	4-3
2005	League Cup	Rangers	1-5

A BUNCH OF QUEENS

While it is proudly remembered that Motherwell inflicted Celtic's record defeat, it is less well known that Motherwell also have the same dubious place in the history books of Queen's Park. The once proud amateurs were still competitive in the top flight of Scottish football by 1930, even if they were no longer challenging for honours. However, at the end of the 1929/30 season they slumped to a 9-0 defeat at Fir Park – a thumping defeat which has never been matched, even as they tumbled down the leagues in the years to come. Ferrier, Dowall and Murdoch grabbed the goals; four, three and two respectively.

THE FIRST RELEGATION...

The future seemed bright with two cups being won in the previous years, but season 1952/53 turned into one of the worst ever. Things were so bad that the first win at Fir Park did not arrive until December and a dismal loss to Aberdeen early in the Scottish Cup meant that survival soon became the only goal. While a win against Queen of the South lifted hopes, two losses to finish ensured the side ended the year in the relegation zone. Motherwell finished only one point behind Airdrie, Falkirk and Raith Rovers, and even Hearts in fourth were only five points better off. Alas, it made no difference and the club had to cope with relegation for the first time.

...THE FIRST PROMOTION...

Motherwell wasted no time in asserting themselves on Division B as they looked to win promotion back to the top league at the first time of asking in 1953/54. Three wins on the trot was a great start to the campaign and although there were a couple of losses the side soon found their stride and were firing in the goals. A 2-1 win over Arbroath ensured manager George Stevenson guided the team to the title and with it promotion. He had saved his job but needed to establish the club in Division A once more as a matter of urgency.

...AND THE FIRST ESCAPE

In season 1954/55 the league campaign started brightly but deteriorated rapidly and a poor finish saw the club land in the relegation places once again. For the first, but not the last time, the fates would intervene favourably to help the side survive. League reconstruction was needed following a disagreement on the use of reserve sides that prompted the top division to expand from 16 clubs to 18. A substantial majority voted in favour of the bottom two clubs, Motherwell and Stirling Albion, retaining their top-flight status and relegation was avoided on a technicality. Despite this, George Stevenson tendered his resignation to end an association with the club lasting over 20 years. Having played a part in the winning of every major domestic honour as player or manager, he will never be forgotten at Fir Park.

BABY COME BACK

While many players leave Fir Park to seek fame and riches elsewhere, many have found the lure of Motherwell too difficult to resist. In the current squad, Stevie Hammell and Keith Lasley both returned following spells in England while Stephen Craigan made his way back via Partick Thistle having originally been released.

TWENTY-20

No Motherwell striker has managed 20 goals in a top-flight season since Willie Pettigrew achieved the feat in 1976/77. While the likes of Tommy Coyne and Chris Porter both went close to the mark by grabbing 18 in all competitions, Willie Falconer topped the list with just five in 1995/96; but in fairness to Willie, he was only signed in January that season! Willie Irvine did manage to hit the magical 20 mark in 1981/82 but he had the benefit of playing against First Division defences as the club stormed towards promotion back to the Premier League.

SELL ON NOT SELL OUT

Many modern-day transfers contain a sell-on clause but the practice is far from new. When Motherwell sold Pat Quinn to Blackpool in 1962, such a clause was included in a transfer already worth £34,000. Quinn had been an integral part of the Ancell Babes team that dazzled Scottish football for a number of years but sadly finished without any trophies to show for their play. His sale, together with the departure of Ian St. John to Liverpool, signalled the end of this particular era at Fir Park.

SHINE A LIGHT

Falkirk were trailing 3-1 at Fir Park on a dark December afternoon when they were granted a reprieve due to floodlight failure and they made the most of their good fortune by winning 2-1 at the second attempt. Remarkably, the two sides were involved in a similar incident, albeit at Brockville, in 1995 when a Scottish Cup tie had to be abandoned. On that occasion, Motherwell finally progressed with a 2-0 win.

PLAYER OF THE YEAR

Ever since Scottish journalists and professionals have respectively named their Player of the Year, no Motherwell representative has ever scooped the accolade for being the best in the top division. Brian McLaughlin won the First Division award from his fellow professionals in the promotion season of 1981/82 while Phil O'Donnell and James McFadden were both later recognised as the best young player.

SIMPLY THE BEST

Many of the great players in world football have turned out at Fir Park, albeit usually for the opposition! One exception who donned the famous claret and amber was George Best who arrived with the San Jose Earthquakes for a friendly in 1981. George played a half for each side allowing him to claim an important role in a comfortable 5-2 win for the Steelmen.

A PLEASING RECORD

Looking through the significant records of Celtic may not normally be interesting reading for Motherwell fans but there is one fact which deserves to be highlighted – their record defeat. Celtic were put to the sword by a remarkable 8-0 scoreline at Fir Park in 1937, as Motherwell ran riot. Alex Stewart was carried shoulder high to the station after grabbing six goals against a Celtic side hampered by two injuries including one to their goalkeeper. A convenient excuse, no doubt!

CAN'T SAY FAIRER THAN THAT

Motherwell qualified for the newly formed Europa League in 2009 despite finishing seventh in the table and exiting both domestic cups early on. The reason was the Fair Play scheme instigated by Uefa to reward sporting clubs that handed Scotland an extra spot in the first qualifying round of the competition. Rather embarrassingly, Motherwell did not even win the domestic Fair Play league but were runners-up to Celtic who had already qualified for the Champions League. St. Mirren challenged for the spot until the closing stages of the season but the good behaviour of Mark McGhee's men triumphed.

IN GEORGE BEST'S ILLUSTRIOUS CAREER HE EVEN PLAYED BRIEFLY FOR MOTHERWELL IN A FRIENDLY MATCH.

"GO FOR IT, ALAN!"

Can four words have ever cost a side the Scottish Cup? The above call, extolling a player to attack the ball in a crowded penalty box, was at the heart of the defensive disaster that allowed Celtic to score a late equaliser against Motherwell in the cup final of 1931. Motherwell had been in control and even though Celtic pulled back a late goal, the Steelmen led 2-1 in the dying minutes and the trophy seemed set for Lanarkshire. Celtic managed one last attack but in response to the 'go for it' instruction both centre-back Alan Craig and goalkeeper Allan McClory dashed for the ball. The defender won the race but the ball skidded off his head and into the unguarded goal. Celtic made the most of their good fortune by winning the replay 4-2.

BENCH WARMER

'Johnny Gahagan on the wing' was a popular song among Motherwell fans but while Gahagan made a big contribution in his 11 years at Fir Park, it was frequently from the bench. He was used as a substitute on an amazing 93 occasions, a record for a Motherwell player.

CLOUD NINE

Motherwell opened season 1962/63 in simply sensational fashion and at half-time in the first game of the League Cup campaign led Falkirk 9-0! Pat Quinn notched four of the goals but somehow Bobby Russell managed to go one better and claim five. The Bairns managed to avoid falling apart completely and even managed a consolation goal in the second half as the match ended 9-1. Unfortunately, Motherwell failed to build on this win and exited the competition at the group stage.

PENALTY HERO

Steve Kirk is well known for his goalscoring exploits but against Hearts in 1988 he found himself between the posts rather than attacking them. Acting as a stand-in goalkeeper, Kirk parried a penalty kick from Wayne Foster and inspired a comeback that allowed the side to escape Tynecastle with a 2-2 draw.

A PROUD RECORD

Despite only winning the championship once in the glory years under Sailor Hunter, the club had a remarkable and proud record of finishing in the top three in eight consecutive seasons. A good campaign which came up a fraction short of being enough to win the first title brought the runners-up spot in 1927, the highest place achieved by the club. The title win of 1932 was the high point, especially as this was the only success enjoyed by a non-Old Firm side between the wars. The level of consistency shown in finishing so high every following year until 1934 was a remarkable achievement.

LOCAL INTRIGUE

When traditional rivals Airdrie hit financial difficulties, Lanarkshire was filled with rumours about their future. According to one national newspaper, Motherwell chairman John Boyle even wanted to buy the grief-stricken team and merge his two clubs into a potential football superpower called Lanarkshire United. The claims were denied by everyone involved although once Airdrie plunged into administration, Motherwell considered buying their ground as the central part of a new youth academy along with renting it out for other matches to create additional income.

ALLY'S ARMY

Ally McLeod is best known for leading Scotland to Argentina to win the 1978 World Cup but he also had a spell in charge of the Steelmen. With the side struggling against the drop in season 1978/79 the Board persuaded McLeod to take over at Fir Park but even the enthusiastic new manager could not save the doomed team and relegation followed. McLeod could only inspire the team to a pair of mid-table finishes in his two full years in charge in the First Division before he left the club in August 1981.

IN FOR A POUND, IN FOR A FIVER

One statistic which stands out in Motherwell's history is the crowd of 11,200 for a Sunday evening game against Dundee United in 1998. John Boyle had just taken over the club and wanted to attract the local public to Fir Park; he slashed prices to £5 for adults and £1 for kids.

A MAN FOR EUROPE

Motherwell began their fifth European campaign in 2009/10 but for several years Jamie Dolan held the unique record of being the only player to appear in every continental game played by the club. He featured in each leg against Katowice, Havnar, Borussia Dortmund and MyPa 47 between 1991 and 1995 in the European Cup Winners' Cup and Uefa Cup and his record only came to an end in 2008 when the side met Nancy.

ON FRIENDLY TERMS

The construction of floodlights at Fir Park sparked an era of friendly matches against sides from all over Europe, and beyond. Djurgardens IF of Sweden were the first non-British side to visit and were promptly defeated 2-1 in 1958, with the likes of Athletic Bilbao, Flamenco, Bahia and Toulouse all coming a cropper in future years. The practice did decline but it was the arrival of Ajax in 1977 that signalled that the time for these games being viewed as genuine challenge matches was over. The club's Board had invested a substantial amount of money to bring the Dutch masters to Scotland but few fans turned up to see iconic players such as Wim Suurbier and Ruud Kroll, who would go on to play in the 1978 World Cup final.

NE'ER DAY NO MORE

Crawling out of bed with a hangover and heading off to the football on January 1st used to be a tradition in Scotland but Motherwell have only played twice on Ne'er Day in the last 17 years. Both games were against Kilmarnock but, as they only produced a 0-0 draw at Rugby Park in 1994 – and a 2-1 home defeat in 1999 – perhaps this is one custom we are better off without! Motherwell's usual opponents for the first foot encounters were Hamilton Academical or Airdrie but on occasion the side have also clashed with St. Mirren, Falkirk, Ayr United, Albion Rovers, Clyde and Partick Thistle. The most unusual opponents on this famous footballing day were Forfar Athletic, who were forced to make the long journey south for a Second Division game in 1969. Both Albion Rovers and Hamilton were also in the league but were paired against each other in Coatbridge, meaning the Loons had to face Motherwell.

CUP WINS: 1952 – SUCCESS AT THE FIFTH ATTEMPT

Perseverance was a virtue finally rewarded when Motherwell collected the Scottish Cup of 1952. The club had endured a love-hate relationship with the tournament since the semi-finals were first reached in 1923. On that occasion, Celtic ended the run and they would prove a frequent thorn in the side of the club in years to come. They defeated Motherwell in two cup finals in the 1930s and Clyde took their turn to give the side a taste of Hampden misery in 1939. After a break enforced by the Second World War, the team needed a few years to get going but reached the cup final again in 1951 to face Celtic – the outcome was an oh so predictable defeat. But, in 1952, the Steelmen finally took the famous old trophy back to Fir Park by hammering Dundee 4-0 thanks to second-half goals from Watson, Redpath, Humphries and Kelly securing the victory, although credit must also go to Willie Kilmarnock who made three goal-line clearances before the break. While the final ended in a comfortable win, the whole cup run was outstanding. Motherwell were not drawn at home at all in the tournament and after beating Forfar Athletic in the first round, the side needed to fight back from two down to win 3-2 at St. Mirren. Dunfermline Athletic were dispatched with a replay in the next round and Rangers suffered the same fate in front of a packed Fir Park. An epic semi-final clash with Hearts needed three games to be settled at Hampden with Motherwell eventually triumphing 3-1 after two 1-1 draws. That meant by the time Willie Kilmarnock lifted the cup the side had played ten games in the competition but such a huge effort was a fitting end to a cup odyssey lasting several decades. The win also meant that Sailor Hunter, the ageing club secretary, was finally able to get his hands on the cup having managed the team to three unsuccessful finals during his time in charge.

MCCLAIR AGAINST THE WORLD

Young attacker Brian McClair made his name in dramatic fashion when he grabbed five goals in successive home games against Rangers and Celtic in early 1983. A hat-trick secured a 3-0 win against the former and a double a 2-1 success over the latter.

AS I WALKED DOWN THE COPLAND ROAD...

One of Motherwell's most famous ever wins came in the Scottish Cup of 1961. The Ancell Babe side, so admired by many, were staring at defeat at home to Rangers when they trailed 2-0, but a dramatic comeback secured a draw and a second chance at Ibrox. A sell-out crowd packed the terraced slopes in Glasgow and although Motherwell took an early lead, the home fans were soon cheered as they led 2-1. What happened then became the stuff of legend. Pat Delaney equalised, Bobby Roberts put the guests in front on the hour mark and further strikes from Ian St. John, and Roberts again produced a sensational 5-2 victory. Motherwell being Motherwell, the next round was lost against the run of play at home to Airdrie but the joy of beating Rangers in such a fashion lives on. There is still a song sung about the win; although sadly it remains the last time Motherwell knocked Rangers out of any cup competition with the last 12 knock-out ties all going the way of the Ibrox club.

HAMMER OF THE OLD FIRM

Dougie Arnott is one of the most popular strikers of recent times at Fir Park and even though he retired in 1998, he is still fondly thought of by Motherwell fans. Originally signed from the juniors by Tommy McLean in the middle of the 1980s, it took some time to break into the starting line-up on a regular basis but his huge work-rate and refusal to give up on lost causes soon made him a favourite. The goals began to flow and he even finished top scorer in the glorious season of 1990/91. Arnott contributed to the cup run but only scored in one game, grabbing two goals in the semi-final replay win over Celtic. That was not overly surprising given his wonderful record of netting against both halves of the Old Firm. Time and time again Arnott scored goals against the Glasgow duo with a notable double bringing a come-from-behind winner at Ibrox in 1993, and a scrambled finish ruined Fergus McCann's first game as Celtic chairman a couple of years later. Dougie was awarded a testimonial match against an Old Firm select in 2008 and he now works as bar manager at Fir Park.

COPLAND
ROAD
STAND

MOTHERWELL'S MANAGERS

The range of time enjoyed – or endured – by the person in the hotseat certainly reflects the development of modern football. Hunter was there for decades and his replacement, George Stevenson, had been a player at the club for over 20 years before moving into the manager's office. Bobby Ancell and Bobby Howitt, his successors, were in charge for ten and eight years, respectively, meaning that from April 1911 to July 1973 the club were led by only four managers, in 62 years; a simply astonishing record which will surely never be matched again. Since that period, only Tommy McLean has been in place for more than five years although Alex McLeish and Terry Butcher both managed four. However, a clear pattern has emerged with several managers failing to last more than one season before giving up or being moved on while those modern managers who do achieve even relative success – like Butcher and McGhee – are soon tempted away to what they perceive to be bigger and better things. In the whole history of the club, only three managers have managed to pick up major silverware with Hunter taking the league in 1932, and Tommy McLean the Scottish Cup in 1991. In between, George Stevenson collected the League Cup in 1950 and the Scottish Cup in 1952. The list of managers even making a major final, but losing, is not much greater as only Terry Butcher could be added to the group! It would be a harsh compiler who refused to extend the role of honour to include Bobby Ancell and Mark McGhee for finishing third, while Alex McLeish guided the team to the runners-up spot in 1995. That gives a total of seven managers out of 20 who have achieved a concrete success at the club; not a huge amount by any means but perhaps greater than would be expected. It certainly shows that Jim Gannon will have a hard job in leading the club in the months ahead, especially given the financial situation he will be forced to work under. It is also apparent that it would be a major shock if Gannon stays at the club long enough to offer the stability of previous years. If things go well, a bigger club will inevitably swoop while neither the Board nor modern managers seem to have the stomach for a long battle through a bad start. An interesting thesis could no doubt be made as to why this change has been made – but that is for another time!

MOTHERWELL'S MANAGERS

Motherwell have had 20 managers in their history, with the first genuine occupant of the post being Sailor Hunter. Hunter has not yet been given the recognition he deserves for his extraordinary spell at the club that lasted for 35 years as manager, and then several more as secretary. He led the club from being a small provincial side to one that won the league championship, and both domestic cups, either side of the Second World War.

Manager	Arrived	Departed
John 'Sailor' Hunter	April 1911	May 1946
George Stevenson	May 1946	May 1955
Bobby Ancell	June 1955	June 1965
Bobby Howitt	March 1965	July 1973
Ian St. John	July 1973	September 1974
Willie McLean	September 1974	December 1977
Roger Hynd	December 1977	November 1978
Ally McLeod	December 1978	August 1981
Davie Hay	August 1981	May 1982
Jock Wallace	June 1982	November 1983
Bobby Watson	November 1983	May 1984
Tommy McLean	June 1984	July 1994
Alex McLeish	July 1994	February 1998
Harri Kampman	February 1998	October 1998
Billy Davies	October 1998	October 2001
Eric Black	October 2001	April 2002
Terry Butcher	April 2002	May 2006
Maurice Malpas	May 2006	June 2007
Mark McGhee	June 2007	June 2009
Jim Gannon	June 2009	Present

STANDING ROOM ONLY

The last official match at Fir Park in which terracing was legally used was against St. Johnstone in 1994. A fine season from Motherwell ended without a spark, though, as the side failed to score one last goal when attacking the end hosting their fans on the north terracing and were defeated 1-0.

CLARET AND AMBER COLOURS TRUE

Though Motherwell now take to the field in a snazzy outfit made up of unique claret and amber colours, this was not always the case. The original colours were blue and though there was a slight change in tone and occasional flirtation with stripes, a simple plain coloured top was used for many years. That changed in 1913 when a claret shirt with amber round the collar area was used for the first time. It took a few more years until, towards the end of the 1920s, a claret band was looped the whole way round an amber body with corresponding hoops going round the arms. The classical Motherwell top had been born and it quickly became as recognisable a feature in Scottish football as Celtic's hoops or Airdrie's diamond. Popular legend claims the colours were adopted from the racing colours of the Duke of Hamilton but sadly this romantic tale is a myth. A more practical solution is the directors wished to cut down on the number of times a change shirt was needed so moved from the common blue to something unique in Scottish football. Bradford City, the only other side in Britain to play in claret and amber, had won the FA Cup in 1911 and although not confirmed, it seems likely that this was the true factor behind the adoption of new colours. In more modern times the hoop has often been reduced to a stripe across the front of the strip or abandoned altogether. The latest kit, made by Canterbury, sees a return to the full loop.

A CROWD ANOMALY

Motherwell's record attendance has been widely recorded as 35,632 for a 1952 cup replay against Rangers – but that figure is actually incorrect. The *Motherwell Times* reported that the stated figure paid their way in to Fir Park for the match but this did not include season ticket holders or those holding complimentary tickets. The total number of fans inside the ground is likely to have exceeded 37,000 but as it is impossible to discover the true number of attendees, the lower figure will continue as the accepted record despite the newspaper reporting 36,800 had previously watched a cup tie with Celtic. The crowd for the Rangers game generated receipts of £2,530 and the fans also went home happy as Motherwell won 2-1 and continued on the road to Hampden, and eventual Scottish Cup glory.

EARNING THEIR SPURS

The introduction of the Texaco Cup in the early 1970s provided Motherwell with a chance to test themselves against some of the top teams in England. Stoke City were dispatched after a penalty shoot-out to set up one of the most famous nights in the club's history. The mighty Tottenham Hotspur came to Fir Park and left with their tails firmly between their legs. In the first meeting between the sides at White Hart Lane, Motherwell lost narrowly but goals from Donnelly and Watson gave the side a credible 3-2 defeat. Spurs were still favourites though and when they opened the scoring in front of a packed Fir Park, they looked set to progress to the next round. Instead, roared on by over 20,000 fans, Motherwell fought back with goals from Herron, Watson and Donnelly – and a sterling performance from MacRae in goals – to claim a sensational victory. Motherwell reached the semi-finals of the tournament but exited at home to Hearts while Spurs took consolation from winning the League Cup that season and the Uefa Cup the following year.

HOT SHOT MCFADYEN

Motherwell's league championship-winning side of 1931/32 contained a number of stars but one of the most spectacular was Willie McFadyen. McFadyen scored at a tremendous rate throughout his time at the club but in this particular year he excelled himself. He grabbed 52 goals in 38 league games to set a Scottish scoring record that still stands to this day, despite the best efforts of more modern strikers such as Brian McClair, Henrik Larsson and Ally McCoist. Even Jimmy McGrory, McFadyen's contemporary, failed to match this record despite finishing with a career average of better than a goal a game.

PENALTY PERFECTION

Some professional footballers find it notoriously difficult to put the ball in the net from 12 yards but Motherwell went through a period of being blessed with two reliable penalty takers who never missed. Shaun Teale did have one scare when Alan Combe saved his effort at Tannadice Park but he was granted a re-take that he converted. Ged Brannan then stepped up to become the regular taker and he also maintained a 100 per cent record during his time at the club.

WINNING WITH YOUR FEET UP

When Motherwell became champions of Scotland in 1932 the title was confirmed when the side were actually enjoying a day off. A backlog of fixtures caused by Rangers reaching the Scottish Cup final meant they still had a few games to play when Motherwell only had one tie remaining. Had Rangers won all of their games and Motherwell lost their final fixture, the Ibrox club may have been able to steal the championship on goal average. In the event, there were no final-day nerves for Motherwell as Rangers could only draw with Clyde meaning the title went to Fir Park with a game to spare!

KINGS OF SPAIN

Motherwell extended both their reputation and finances by undertaking a number of lucrative tours in the 1920s and 1930s. The most famous of these was the first that involved the club travelling to Spain and taking on the might of Real Madrid and Barcelona (and Swansea Town!) for the King of Spain Cup. Swansea were dispatched 4-3 and when goals from Ferrier, Thackery and Hutchieson produced a victory against Madrid, the club were on the verge of a glorious success. Barcelona did manage to hold on for a 2-2 draw against the Steelmen but the side from Lanarkshire still went home with the large trophy. Further games in the tour saw fixtures with Athletic Bilbao, Celta Vigo and then Red Star Olympique.

SPARE A THOUGHT

The club has been blessed with several fans who seem only too delighted to go above and beyond the call of duty in supporting the team. One hardy bunch set out to see the first-ever European game played by the side against Katowice in Poland in the 1991/92 season but attempted to travel there by bus. Hours stretched into days but due to a hold up in travelling through the former East Germany, the dedicated fans only made it to the ground in time to see the last eight minutes of a 2-0 defeat. They certainly claimed their place in the history of this great club although no doubt they would all wish to have achieved that through other means!

GOING DUTCH

At the end of the 1980s, and at the start of the 1990s, there became a trend in Scottish football to import players from Holland. The Dutch contingent were perceived as being technically strong while offering better value for money than their Scottish counterparts. Luc Nijholt was the first to arrive from Old Boys in Switzerland for £100,000 in 1990. His uncompromising style quickly made him a favourite with the fans and despite breaking his leg in his first season, he returned to play an important part in winning the Scottish Cup. Nijholt moved on to Swindon Town before returning to the Netherlands where he began his managerial career with Telstar before working as a coach with AZ Alkmaar and Red Bull Salzburg. Despite expressing an interest in becoming Motherwell manager, Luc has not yet managed an official return to Fir Park although should this eventually happen it would be a very popular appointment.

THE DARKEST DAY

Motherwell have suffered several disappointments on the pitch but it was an off the field event which caused the support the most grief in recent years. In April 2002 fans woke up to newspaper headlines proclaiming the 'Well had run dry and that the club was heading for bankruptcy. As the news developed, it eventually became clear that it was 'only' administration that beckoned but the complete failure of the club's finances was still a shock. The fans quickly rallied round to raise money and this eventually led to the formation of the Motherwell Supporters Trust. After a couple of years under the guiding hand of Bryan Jackson, of accountancy firm PKF, the club was able to make a deal with creditors to exit interim administration, largely due to owner John Boyle waiving his right to the lion's share of the available pot.

ON PROGRAMME

Motherwell's first-ever programme was issued at the start of the 1948/49 season for a home game against Rangers. Priced at just 2d, readers were able to take home a value for money memento of a 1-1 draw secured courtesy of a goal by Davie Mathie. The Motherwell programme has been a fixture every season since and in 2008/09 picked up a number of awards after an impressive revamp.

AT LONG LAST

Football frequently throws up hoodoos where one team seems destined to fail forever against another. Though Celtic beating Motherwell is not perhaps that much of a surprise, the Hoops seemed to hold an Indian sign over the Steelmen when it came to meetings at Hampden. Celtic were too strong the very first time Motherwell reached the Scottish Cup semi-final in 1923 as they triumphed 2-0 at Ibrox. Twice in the early 1930s, Motherwell met Celtic in Scottish Cup finals only to lose narrowly (1-0) in 1931 and throw it away in 1933 to lose in a replay. After the war, Motherwell took some time to build up the team again but reached the Scottish Cup final in 1951 only to lose to Celtic yet again. While in 'B' Division in 1954, Motherwell managed to reach the semi-finals only to meet a familiar end against Celtic in another replay – the fate was repeated in 1965. Exactly 20 years later, Motherwell were en route to the First Division title but the chance of Scottish Cup glory was ruined by Celtic in, shock of shocks, a replay. The League Cup was not such a regular source of pain but in 1986 Celtic still managed to kill the latest Hampden dream with a penalty shoot-out. By the time Motherwell reached the 1991 Scottish Cup final – and were unlucky not to turn a 0-0 draw into a late victory – a replay against Celtic had become a thing to fear. Celtic led 1-0 and 2-1 but this Motherwell side were made of stern stuff and Dougie Arnott's second of the game levelled things before dream goals from Colin O'Neill and Steve Kirk settled the tie. Motherwell went on to win the cup that year but the Celtic jinx at Hampden had not been broken for long. In the next meeting, the 2006 League Cup semi-final, Motherwell lost 2-1 despite going a goal up early on. The more things change...

FANS WITH TYPEWRITERS

Motherwell were a little late to join the fanzine craze of the 1980s and it was not until late 1989 that the first issue of *Waiting for the Great Leap Forward* appeared on the streets. The fanzine has survived many changes but is still going to this day under the guidance of latest editor Chris Hutton.

NET BUSTER

As with many clubs, the top scorer in the history of Motherwell did his work a long time ago. One of Sailor Hunter's earliest signings was that of centre forward Hugh Ferguson from Parkhead Juniors. He started his senior career as he meant to continue, quickly finding the net against Raith Rovers early in the 1916-17 wartime season. Over the next nine years, Ferguson dominated the centre forward position and racked up a tally of around 283 goals although the exact number is not known for sure. During his spell at Fir Park the club managed a top-three finish and reached the semi-finals of the cup. He moved on from Motherwell to join Cardiff City and was equally successful in the valleys. The greatest moment in his career came in 1927 when he scored the goal that saw City defeat Arsenal in the FA Cup final and take the trophy out of England for the only time. Ferguson returned to Scotland with Dundee but was hampered by injury and failed to cope with the expectations placed upon him. He committed suicide aged just 31.

BOOK IN HAND

For many years, starting in 1922, Motherwell had the quaint tradition of publishing the *Motherwell Handbook*. Originally a small pocket-sized guide, it contained all the information needed by anyone interested in the club in the coming year, including the fixtures for the season. The tradition died out by the early 1980s. The handbook made a brief comeback – in the classic style used between 1938 and 1965 – between 1995 and 1998 but due to a combination of factors, such as the continual improvement of the match programme and now the internet providing information at the touch of a button, this famous institution has become obsolete.

CONSISTENCY BREEDS SUCCESS

Motherwell's cup success in 1952 was built on the consistency of team selection. Though Donald McLeod deputised in the midfield in the first round, Charlie Cox resumed his usual position for the next game. From the second round against St. Mirren to the final with Dundee, and all the replays, the following line-up produced the goods: Johnston, Kilmarnock, Shaw, Cox, Paton, Redpath, Sloan, Humphries, Kelly, Watson and Aitkenhead.

GONE BUT NOT FORGOTTEN: PHIL O'DONNELL

On December 29th 2007, Motherwell captain Phil O'Donnell collapsed on the pitch during a game against Dundee United. Despite being rushed to Wishaw General Hospital, he died of heart failure that evening. There was an immediate outpouring of grief not only from the Motherwell staff and support, but from all over Scotland. Phil was hugely respected not only for his abilities on the park but as a man, and it seems no one in the intense world of Scottish professional football had a bad word to say about him. The Main Stand at Fir Park was renamed in his honour. Phil broke into the Motherwell team in 1990 and the combination of his lung-bursting runs and his obvious talent soon endeared him to the Motherwell support. Manager Tommy McLean used him sparingly at first but by the Scottish Cup final of 1991, he was a fixture in the midfield. He wasn't overawed by the big occasion and his first-ever goal, a courageous diving header, capped a large contribution to Motherwell's first triumph in 39 years. A couple of disappointing seasons followed for the club as they failed to build on the cup win but Phil was still named Scottish PFA Young Player of the Year in 1992, an award he would also collect in 1994. The fruit of several years' labour by Tommy McLean came in season 1993/94 when a magnificent Motherwell side finished third and came agonisingly close to winning the title. O'Donnell was now the midfield star and moved to Celtic for £1.75m early in the next season – a club record fee that still stands to this day. Injuries were beginning to take their toll, though, and despite winning the league championship and another Scottish Cup with the Parkhead side, Phil was unable to add to the one Scottish cap he had collected while at Motherwell for making a 15-minute substitute appearance against Switzerland at Pittodrie. A spell at Sheffield Wednesday was ruined by more injury problems and Phil returned to Fir Park in 2003 under Terry Butcher. Few would have expected Phil to be anything more than a bit-part player at this stage of his career, but he complemented the younger players and helped the team to Hampden again in the 2005 League Cup final. At the time of his death, Phil was still in the midfield as Mark McGhee's side stormed six points clear in third place on the way to claiming a Uefa Cup spot.

SUMMER SUN

Among the many honours picked up by the club are two Summer Cups from 1944 and 1965. The success at Hampden in 1944 gave the club a boost following three cup final defeats at the same venue before the war. By 1965 the tournament had declined a little as both Rangers and Celtic failed to enter. Motherwell battled through to the two-legged final and a 1-0 defeat at Tannadice was not enough to overturn a 3-1 win at Fir Park. The cup was an ample reward for the club who had gone so close to major honours in the Bobby Ancell era that had ended mere weeks before.

AWAY AT HOME

Motherwell playing 'away' at Fir Park is a strange concept but it happened twice in the 2007/08 season when the club 'visited' Gretna. Raydale failed to meet SPL requirements so a deal was struck to use Fir Park. However, Motherwell retained the use of the home dressing room when they met Gretna for the first-ever time in August 2007. The 'Well triumphed 2-1 on that occasion and after defeating the Border side 3-0 in a home tie at Fir Park, the last away trip also produced a win, by 3-1. Gretna playing at Fir Park boosted the club finances but a heavy price was paid in terms of the pitch. It became one of the worst in Scotland and contributed hugely to a fixture backlog as the weather dipped at the turn of the year.

SO CLOSE YET SO FAR

No Scottish side had ever progressed in European competition after losing the first leg at home but Motherwell went agonisingly close in 1995. Finnish part-timers MyPa 47, containing future stars Joonas Kolkka and Sami Hyypia, were already well into their season when they hammered a rusty Motherwell 3-1 at Fir Park but things were different just two weeks later. Motherwell scored in each half of the return leg but when Lee McCulloch shot just past the post in the dying seconds the dream was over. Motherwell exited on away goals for the second time in four European ties but they would soon have another crack at recovering a home deficit to make history...

THE FIRST GLORY

Motherwell picked up their first of many Lanarkshire Cups when they defeated Albion Rovers in the final of the 1895 event. Special trains were organised to ferry fans to Airdrie for the contest which Motherwell won 7-3. A large crowd congregated at the town cross to wait for the side to return and a long night of celebrations followed. Motherwell went on to win the tournament – first played in the 1879/80 season and won by Stonelaw – a record 32 times before it was discontinued after 1995/96. Periodically there are calls for the competition to be brought back but with fans already asked to pay a premium for modern football and Motherwell, usually, being a substantial way ahead of the other local teams, it seems unlikely this will happen.

TICKETS PLEASE

While all-ticket matches are an inconvenience most fans are now used to, it was not always so. The first-ever ticket-only match at Fir Park was the Scottish Cup quarter-final of 1939 against Celtic. The 31,000 who remembered to buy their tickets in advance were rewarded with a 3-1 win thanks to a double from McCulloch and another goal from Stevenson. Motherwell defeated Aberdeen in a semi-final replay but came up short in the final, losing 4-0 to Clyde at Hampden Park. The outbreak of the Second World War a few months later meant that the Scottish Cup was not put up for grabs again for several years, meaning Clyde, not Motherwell, hold the record for longest possession of the trophy.

BELIEVE IT OR NOT

The emergence of the magnificent Ancell Babes prompted the Motherwell Board to renovate Fir Park and increase the capacity. In 1959 the existing terracing was improved and extended which enabled the ground to hold a massive 40,000, but sadly this mark was never reached. The first game after the renovations were completed attracted over 13,000 to watch St. Johnstone, something that seems remarkable now but was actually a little disappointing at the time. The last great crowd inside the ground was 26,700 against St. Mirren in a 1977 Scottish Cup tie but by then even that number had to hold their breath to squeeze into the famous old stadium.

EXPLAINING THE GAP

In an age of almost identikit football stadiums across the country, Fir Park still retains a certain character. Arguably, it is the character of a ground beyond its best and in almost constant need of repair, but it is unique and looks nothing like anything else in Scotland. One of the most distinguishing marks is the long pylon protruding out of the Phil O'Donnell Stand which dates from the reconstruction of the small Main Stand in the early 1960s. The stand was originally intended to go the length of the pitch but complaints from the owners of houses in neighbouring Fir Park Street meant it was restricted. Motherwell eventually managed to buy some of the problematic property several years later but by then an increase in capacity would not bring a worthwhile return on the investment. At the time the new Main Stand was built, it was alleged some Motherwell fans chose not to use it as it was believed to have been funded by the sale of Pat Quinn and Ian St. John. In reality both these players would have wanted to leave for bigger and better things regardless so extending the stand was probably a sign of ambition. The stand was then renamed in honour of former captain Phil O'Donnell following his death at the end of 2007.

MADE FOR TELEVISION

Motherwell's first venture onto BBC television arrived in 1960 when cameras filmed highlights of a match against Hibernian. The watching viewers were not disappointed as they were presented with a seven-goal thriller – although sadly it was visitors Hibs who grabbed the points in a 4-3 win.

ON THE BOYLE

Motherwell were facing financial ruin in the early 1980s when local butcher John Chapman took over as chairman and majority owner. He guided the club back into the black off the field and under the stewardship of Tommy McLean, the Scottish Cup was collected on the park. However, when the economically conservative Chapman sold his shares in 1998, John Boyle took over with a new business plan. Sadly, his increased investment in terms of wages and transfer fees backfired under the leadership of Pat Nevin and the club plunged into administration in 2002.

SHAKE HANDS! KISS BABIES! VOTE MOTHERWELL!

Remarkably, when Motherwell turned professional in 1893 there was immediate concern about finding enough games to bring in money to pay the players. With the chicken and egg conundrum well and truly sorted – the professionals were there before a real league to play in existed – attention turned to creating a Lanarkshire league of elite local clubs. That was not a particularly satisfying plan but the decision of the Scottish League to expand in size to include a second division was a perfect solution. The league wanted to tap into locations like Lanarkshire, Tayside and Edinburgh so after a successful election, Motherwell joined nine other clubs, including Hibernian, Partick Thistle and Morton, in the 1893/94 Scottish Second Division. Season 1894/95 saw Motherwell finish second but as promotion and relegation were decided by votes rather than points, another year in the lower league beckoned. Motherwell made the ambitious move to the new Fir Park stadium in 1895 and although there were still occasional problems the club was becoming a force in the lower league. When Dundee proposed to increase the top division to 14 teams – they, presumably for selfish reasons, wanted to include a newly formed Aberdeen side – Motherwell saw their chance to pounce. It is probable that other local teams were courted and the west central mafia ensured that Motherwell and Airdrie were elected with 11 and eight votes respectively while Aberdeen were left out in the cold with only five. Season 1903/04, the first in the top flight, proved to be as dismal as expected despite the club trying to support its rapid expansion by becoming a limited company in 1903. This failed to stop the rot on the pitch but the canvassers were on the ball again as Motherwell successfully applied for re-election in 1905 after finishing bottom of the table. This was common practice at the time but it would not be the first occasion Motherwell would benefit from boardroom decisions. Off-field matters saved the club from relegation in 1955, 1986 and 2003 and avoided the necessity of a potentially tricky relegation play-off against Airdrie in 1998. However, it is arguable that luck is not the issue but more what happens after it that counts. St. Mirren were saved from relegation in 1991 but where Motherwell have made the most of breaks like this by stabilising and improving, the Buddies promptly finished bottom the next year and duly spent the vast majority of the next 20 years in the First Division.

FASTEST MAN IN THE WEST

There's something about signing foreign players which is just something a bit more exotic than their Scottish counterparts. When Namibian international forward Eliphas Shivute signed in 1997, he looked like the answer to the prayers of the fans but sadly things never really got going for him at Fir Park. Despite being well built and fast enough to give Usain Bolt a fright in the 100 metres, actually playing football was a bit more difficult. He did score a diving header on his debut at Ibrox but only found the net twice more before being released after making 24 appearances.

THE SMACK OF IRONY

Andy Roddie was Alex McLeish's first signing after he took over as manager but despite playing 55 games for the club he left with only one goal at Fir Park to his name. What makes this record even worse is that his solitary goal came for Aberdeen when he netted in a 3-3 draw. Despite a reasonable amount of talent and pace, Roddie failed to win over the Motherwell fans and eventually left to pursue his career in Sweden.

THREE'S A CROWD

One of the low moments in Scottish international football came in 1961 when England won the Auld Enemy clash 9-3 at Wembley. Motherwell had to take some share of the blame as three players from Fir Park – Bert McCann, Pat Quinn and Ian St. John – all started. St John, at least, had the consolation of playing in wins over England in each of the next two seasons but neither McCann nor Quinn would play for their country again. It would be over 30 years until three Motherwell players appeared in the same Scotland side again when Brian Martin, Paul Lambert and Rob McKinnon all played in the 0-0 draw against Japan in the Kirin Cup of 1995.

SENT TO COVENTRY

Though the South Stand had been in use for some time, English club Coventry City came north to play at Fir Park in a glamour opening tie in 1993. Goals from Ally Graham and Steve Kirk produced a 2-1 win.

DESPITE GUIDING THE TEAM TO A RUNNERS-UP SPOT IN THE LEAGUE, ALEX MCLEISH IS NOT POPULAR WITH THE 'WELL FANS.

A LOSING HAT-TRICK

Fir Park has seen many sensational games but one which sticks out is the visit of Aberdeen in 1999. The Dons had struggled to score goals all season and had only managed one point from their nine games to this point and with Motherwell not faring that much better a tight contest was expected. What happened was anything but and was even more shocking when it is considered that Andy Goram and Jim Leighton, two of the finest goalkeepers Scotland has produced, were at either end of the park! A remarkable first-half display of inept defending allowed Aberdeen to take a 4-2 lead and when they made it 5-2 then 6-3 the game seemed to be in the bag. Motherwell refused to stop fighting but despite pulling the score back to 5-6 the points were lost. John Spencer can feel particularly hard done by on this occasion as he scored an excellent hat-trick only to still end up on the losing side. Robbie Winters also bagged a treble for Aberdeen while Don Goodman and Shaun Teale contributed the other 'Well goals.

A BIG KIDD-ER

Hearts fans still break into cold sweats at the very mention of Albert Kidd but while he is famous for one particular game, he was actually a former Motherwell player. He had a good scoring record in over 50 First Division appearances but chose to move north to Dundee. Eventually his moment of glory came in the last game of the 1985/86 season when his two late goals ensured the league title went to Celtic rather than Hearts, who were left crying after failing to claim the draw needed for the championship.

AND ON THE OTHER SIDE OF TANNADICE STREET

At Tannadice the old main stand is now named after legendary Dundee United manager Jerry Kerr. He was the driving force which transformed the side from being a middling club in the lower league to one which would make a massive impact on Europe under the stewardship of his successor Jim McLean. Kerr's time as a player at Fir Park was decidedly less impressive though as he failed to displace the wonderful Andy Paton and he left after only making four appearances.

DROPPED FOR DROPPING

There are many famous stories about Tommy McLean imposing his iron discipline on the team but John Gardiner paid a high price for his error in the Scottish Cup. A bumper crowd of over 15,000 turned up at Fir Park for a quarter-final replay against Hearts on a stormy night in March 1987 but Gardiner effectively ended his Motherwell career when he failed to gather a cross which John Colquhoun poked home for the only goal. Gardiner did play in the next league game but was promptly dropped and then never featured for the team again. Cammy Duncan took over for most of the next season but the permanent solution was provided instead by Ally Maxwell. He seized his chance in December 1988 and kept his spot for over 100 consecutive games, a run which ended with heroics in the 1991 cup final.

YOU SPIN ME RIGHT ROUND

The public address system was manned by James Adams for several decades after the war. Club minutes note that in early 1970 he was awarded with a complimentary stand ticket for life as a gift for his retirement.

GOING ON TOUR

Motherwell supplemented gate money by going on a number of lucrative foreign tours in the 1920s and 1930s.

1927	Spain
1928	South America
1931	South Africa
1932	France
1934	South Africa and Rhodesia

NAMES FROM THE PAST

Motherwell's first ever national league campaign in 1893/94 featured contests with the long forgotten Abercorn, Cowlairs, Port Glasgow, Glasgow Thistle and Northern while the Scottish Cup that season threw up ties against Airdriehill and Burnbank Swifts. More familiar names the team faced were Clyde, Partick Thistle, Hibs and Morton.

WHAT A DIFFERENCE A YEAR MAKES

After leading Motherwell to a third-placed finish in 2007/08, manager Mark McGhee was subject to an approach from Hearts. Negotiations led to him being in a London airport about to board a plane for discussions with the Hearts chairman but a last minute change of heart prompted McGhee to stay at Motherwell. However, after failing to build on the success of his first season almost exactly one year later McGhee decided to move to Aberdeen. He was not the first Motherwell manager to endure long speculation over his future – several years earlier Alex McLeish elected to stay at Fir Park having been refused permission to speak to Hibernian but when the Easter Road vacancy came up for a second time, he made it clear he wanted to leave and was allowed to do so. It probably says a lot about football fans that despite McLeish reaching second, and McGhee third, large sections of the support do not remember them fondly.

PRESTON ILLUMINATIONS

Fir Park had floodlights installed in the mid-1950s and the club approached Blackpool to play a glamour friendly as the first match under the new beams. The Seasiders were not available so their near neighbours, Preston North End, took their place. They made the most of the occasion by winning 3-2 – inspired by the great Tom Finney – and they even contributed to the contest by scoring an own goal! That meant Stuart Brown had the honour of becoming the first Motherwell player to score under the new lights.

QUICK OFF THE MARK

The quickest-ever goal scored in a Scotland international career was netted by Willie Pettigrew in 1976. He was only on the pitch for two minutes of his debut against Switzerland in a Hampden friendly when he opened the scoring with what turned out to be the only goal of the game. Pettigrew made a further four appearances for his country and scored another goal against Wales. All of his caps came as a Motherwell player, although both honours he won, two League Cups, happened with Dundee United. Later in his career, Pettigrew played for Hearts, Morton and Hamilton Academical but he is most commonly associated with the Steelmen.

MARK McGHEE TURNED DOWN HEARTS, BUT OPTED TO LEAVE FOR ABERDEEN IN 2009

SIX PACK

Motherwell fans have always enjoyed a special kind of banter with the Hearts support which made one victory in December 2002 all the sweeter. Terry Butcher was in charge of a makeshift squad and a run of one point from 33 meant relegation was a serious threat. That seemed miles away when a sensational performance by James McFadden, in which he scored two and set up another pair, produced a fantastic 6-1 win.

MOTHERWELL'S FIRST CUP-WINNING CAPTAIN

The 'cup battlers' of manager George Stevenson benefitted from a number of leaders on the park. One was Andy Paton, who captained the club in the 1950 League Cup Final triumph and defeat in the 1951 Scottish Cup Final, but he had given up that role by the time the club reached a second successive cup final in 1952. Instead it was full-back Willie Kilmarnock who had the honour of leading the team up the steps to collect the famous trophy after a 4-0 victory against Dundee. Kilmarnock had certainly played a captain's part in the final by making three goal-line clearances in a first half dominated by the opposition before four second-half goals won the day. Kilmarnock was a true Motherwell man who made over 450 league appearances after joining from Renfrew Juniors in 1939 and staying until 1956. Along with collecting winners' and losers' medals in both domestic cups, he also represented Scotland in a wartime international and the Scottish League against Ireland. Ironically, after leaving Fir Park on a free transfer he moved to local rivals Airdrie. He actually captained them against Motherwell in a Ne'er Day derby but even the help of a man of Kilmarnock's stature could not help the hapless Diamonds avoid a 2-0 defeat. Willie died aged 87 in June 2009, a legend in both the corridors of Motherwell FC and his hometown of Irvine.

FASHION PARADE

Along with the famous claret and amber, Motherwell have also lined up in stranger colours; brown shirts and an Inter Milan style blue and black were used on one-offs. Away kits have also heavily featured white, blue and, in the middle of the 1990s, luminous yellow.

FLYING THE FLAG

Along with being awarded a trophy, one quaint tradition of the Scottish leagues is that the winners are presented with a league flag for their efforts. The saltire comes in the colours of the winning club but despite only being awarded one flag for being champions of Scotland, the club no longer has it in its possession. The exact status of the championship flag of 1931/32 is uncertain but the most popular theory is that it was given to a bowling club in South Africa as a memento of a tour in 1934. In retrospect, this was regrettable although perhaps it just reflected the strength of the club at the time that leading figures felt so confident more titles would follow that such an important piece of history could be given away!

IF THE CAP FITS

Motherwell were first honoured with a player receiving international recognition from Scotland in 1910. George Robertson was picked to join the national team for a fixture against Wales at Rugby Park and played his part in a 1-0 win for the home side. He managed to pick up another three international caps in the years ahead in wins against Wales and Northern Ireland and defeat to England at Wembley.

THE FANTASTIC FINN

Though Finnish manager Harri Kampman would arrive at Motherwell in 1998, there was already an immensely popular compatriot of his at Fir Park. Simo Valikari was a tough-tackling midfielder who arrived from Finn Pa in 1997 and instantly impressed on his debut against Aberdeen. Ominously, he spurned a late chance to turn a 2-2 draw into a win when he miskicked completely on the edge of the box which would set the tone for his 'Well career. Despite contributing hugely to the midfield with his defensive abilities, he failed to find the net on a single occasion despite making more than 100 appearances for the club – but ironically enough he promptly scored for Derby having moved south on a free transfer! He held the honour of being Motherwell's most capped player when he bettered George Stevenson's 12 caps for Scotland although he himself has since been trumped by Northern Ireland international Stephen Craigan.

CUPS WINS: 1950 – THE ONLY LEAGUE CUP

The Second World War put the final nail in the lid of Motherwell's glory years of the 1930s although in fairness the club had been on the slide since throwing away the title in 1934. Recovering from that blow proved too much and the team only managed 12th in 1939 – by far the lowest position since 1925 – although some consolation was gained from reaching the cup final that year. After the war, legendary manager Sailor Hunter stood down and was replaced by one of his own players, George Stevenson. Unlike the title challenging days of 20 years before, George could only manage to maintain a solid position in the middle of the table in the league but after a few years in charge produced one of the finest cup sides in Scotland. Several finals were reached in the early part of the 1950s and the first of these Hampden appearances produced silverware. The side had struggled to make an impression on the new League Cup tournament and had actually failed to even make it out of the group stage in four attempts. That changed in 1950 when home and away wins over Airdrie and Partick Thistle, and a share of the spoils with Hearts in the form of a home win and away defeat, were enough to ensure progression to the two-legged quarter-finals. Drawing Celtic next seemed like a blow but a sensational performance at Parkhead produced a 4-1 win which included the added help of an own goal. Despite the second leg resulting in a home defeat, the 1-0 reverse was not enough to prevent Motherwell taking a place in the semi-finals against Ayr United. An up and down game at Ibrox looked to be heading to the west coasters until Willie Watters and Charlie Aitkenhead both completed doubles in the last six minutes to set up a final against Hibs. At this point Hibernian had a tremendously strong team and were heavy favourites to lift the trophy. A strong Motherwell defence was successful in repelling the Hibs attack and this proved to be the foundation of a dramatic win. Archie Kelly, Jim Forrest and Watters all found the net in the second half to spark wild celebrations in Motherwell as the club claimed only its second-ever major trophy. No doubt there would have been partying long into the night although an official celebration did not take place until January, when the Provost hosted a dinner at the town hall.

DO OR DIE

Back in the old days, cup ties used to be settled over numerous replays rather than extra time and penalty kicks. Normally a neutral venue was used from the third attempt onwards. Motherwell's first clash of this nature took place in 1899 and the last in 1986. Here is a complete list:

1899	SC Q2	Carfin Emmett	Douglas Park	3-2
1900	SC Q1	Wishaw United	Douglas Park	3-1
1912	SC 2	Hibs	Celtic Park	1-2
1920	SC 2	Ayr United	Celtic Park	3-1
1920	SC 3	Partick Thistle	Ibrox	1-2
1952	SC Semi	Hearts	Hampden	3-1
1955	LC Quarter	St. Johnstone	Ibrox	2-0
1969	LC Quarter	Morton	Fir Park	1-0
1973	LC Quarter	Celtic	Celtic Park	2-3
1976	SC Quarter	Hibs	Ibrox	2-1
1986	SC 4	Brechin	Tannadice	2-0

THE BEST FORM OF DEFENCE CAN BE DEFENCE

Tommy McLean frequently drew criticism from opponents for the defensive style of play his team employed but on one memorable occasion in 1986 he got the tactics spot on at Ibrox. After defending almost the whole game, Ray Farmingham scored a diving header completely against the run of play to leave Rangers manager Graeme Souness apoplectic. Funnily enough Souness did not see anything wrong with employing similar defensively minded tactics when taking his side abroad in Europe!

SUPER SUB

Angus Moffat made history by being the first-ever Motherwell player used as a substitute. Replacements were allowed from season 1966/67 and Moffat came on in the first game of the League Cup campaign. He added a flourish to his place in the record books by also becoming the first 'Well player to score from the bench, but it was not enough to prevent a 2-1 defeat at Dunfermline Athletic.

A CLOSE SHAVE

While league reconstruction now seems to happen every few years in a usually mistaken attempt to freshen up Scottish football, there was a time when it was not so common. From 1906 there had been at least 16 teams in the First Division, sometimes going as high as 20 in the years before the Second World War, but a radical new plan was announced in the mid-1970s to slice the number of top flight clubs from 18 to just ten. That meant season 1974/75 was a very nervous affair for several mid-table clubs who all of a sudden faced the prospect of being relegated when no danger had previously existed. With just six points separating Ayr United in seventh and Partick Thistle in 13th, the fight went right to the wire but Motherwell managed to secure the tenth and final spot in the new Premier League thanks to a last day 3-1 win at home to Dumbarton with goals from Jim Miller, Bobby Graham and Jim McIlwraith. The change from two large divisions to three tighter leagues was supposed to focus the quality at the upper end. Whether or not that happened is up for debate but there is less argument that the switch imposed a solid ceiling on the ambitions of smaller clubs. In the years leading up to the reconstruction teams like Arbroath, Cowdenbeath, Dumbarton and East Fife had all featured in the highest level of Scottish football – something which is surely unthinkable now.

IF IT WASN'T FOR BAD LUCK

As a reserve goalkeeper it can be hard to keep yourself fit and focussed waiting for a chance to play that may well never come. Back-up keeper Dick Hamilton experienced that for five years between 1947 and 1952 and though he proved to be an able deputy for John Johnston, he was cursed with bad luck. He was actually given a run in the side for the 1950 League Cup march to Hampden but despite having played in every game up to the semi-finals, he was injured for the big day and missed out on a winner's medal from the triumph over Hibs. Hamilton was a good servant to the club under the circumstances but was eventually given a free transfer to let him search for first-team football after making 36 league appearances.

A FINE HONOUR

One of Motherwell's more spectacular post-war tours took place in 1976 when the club played a series of matches in central and South America. A pair of games was played in Haiti against Voilet and Racing, which produced a win and a loss, and one in Colombia against Santa Fe, a defeat, but the most memorable may have been the first match against Toluca in the fantastic Estadio Azteca in Mexico City. This famous venue, with a capacity of over 100,000, had witnessed Carlos Alberto hoist the World Cup aloft for Brazil six years earlier and would also host the 1986 World Cup Final. It is probably fair to say that Ian Taylor's goal in Motherwell's 2-1 defeat is not the most famous in the history of the ground!

A HELPING HAND

Own goals in football bring a superb *Schadenfreude* and Motherwell have benefitted a lot over the recent years with opposition players giving a helping hand. Here is a complete list since the turn of the century:

Player	Game	Season
Darren Dods	Motherwell 4-0 St. Johnstone	2000/01
Paul Kane	Motherwell 1-2 St. Johnstone	2001/02
Frazer Wright	Stranraer 0-4 Motherwell	2002/03
Mathias Doumbe	Hibs 3-3 Motherwell	2003/04
Emanuel Dorado	Livingston 0-5 Motherwell	2004/05
Andy Tod	Motherwell 2-1 Dunfermline	2004/05
Alan Combe	Motherwell 1-1 Kilmarnock	2004/05
Marvin Andrews	Rangers 4-1 Motherwell	2004/05
Michael Hart	Aberdeen 2-1 Motherwell	2006/07
Marius Zaliukas	Hearts 1-2 Motherwell	2007/08
Alan McManus	Motherwell 1-4 Celtic	2007/08

BEST OF THE BEST

As a celebration of its tenth anniversary, the SPL conducted a poll to find the best goal ever scored in the latest incarnation of the Scottish top flight. Remarkably, the honour was won by a Motherwell goal with Jim Hamilton taking the plaudits for a sensational volley against Celtic in 2006.

JUST A BAD IDEA

When glamorous teams from abroad flocked to Fir Park to play floodlit friendly matches in the 1950s and 1960s, Motherwell fans turned out in force to see them. However, the decision to take on IFK Gothenburg, a team in the middle of their own pre-season, in March 2000 showed beyond all doubt that the era for these games was gone. Only a couple of thousand bothered to turn up to watch a deathly boring 0–0 draw as each side was more focussed on the challenges ahead.

A DEADLY DUO (1)

There are some strike duos which the very thought of is enough to see fans through hard times which arrive later. One such combination for Motherwell played together in the middle of the 1970s when Bobby Graham and Willie Pettigrew terrorised defences the length and breadth of the country. Pettigrew, the younger man, possessed greyhound-like pace and was a natural finisher. Signed in 1973 from East Kilbride Thistle, he broke into the side in 1974 and by the time he left in 1979 he had a sensational strike record of 80 goals from less than 160 league starts. Graham, on the other hand, was a wilier operator and frequently assisted on Pettigrew's goals but could also find the net himself and notched 37 goals from 132 league games. Alas, as often seems to happen at Motherwell, a famous team or player was left without major honours to show for their time at Fir Park. The side managed a fourth-place finish in 1976, and lost a couple of cup semi-finals, but that was the height of what they achieved.

THE IMPACT OF BOSMAN

It is now natural to assume that players can move freely from club to club on the expiration of their contracts but it was not always thus. The Bosman ruling changed the way football functioned for all clubs, arguably especially for those middle-of-the-road teams like Motherwell, and there was an immediate impact. In the summer of 1996, the first after the court decision, internationals Paul Lambert and Rob McKinnon left the club for free to try their luck with Borussia Dortmund in Germany and Twente Enschede in the Netherlands.

THE LEFT BACK PHENOMENON

The number ten jersey is cherished all across South America and up the road from Motherwell in Glasgow, the number seven is loved by Celtic fans. At Motherwell if such an honorary number exists it is the decidedly less sexy... three – the figure worn by the left-back, at least before squad numbers made a mockery of such fine traditions. The Motherwell hall of fame in this position stretches all the way back to 1930 when Welsh international Ben Ellis was signed and made the position his own. He played a huge part in the championship win of 1932 and stayed in place until the war. His service was deemed suitable to make him one of the few players to have one of the streets around Fir Park named after him. During the hostilities, Archie Shaw was snapped up from Wishaw Juniors and when football resumed he formed a legendary full-back partnership with Willie Kilmarnock on the other side of the park. Shaw picked up winners' medals in both domestic cups and although he intended to step down from the first team in 1955, he made a brief comeback in the first half of the 1957/58 season. There was then a ten-year gap before the next hero was introduced in 1968 when Joe Wark made his debut. Although Wark would only collect one winner's medal, from the 1969 B Division championship, he was a fixture in the Motherwell side for several years, playing 469 games – a post-war record. Wark is still the only player to have been awarded two testimonials; one against West Bromwich Albion in 1978 and a second against an Old Firm select in 1985. In his final seasons Joe was not a regular but he stayed at the club. In 1984 a young left-back, Tom Boyd, was coming through the ranks. He played a part in winning the First Division in 1985 and by the time of the Scottish Cup triumph in 1991, Boyd was club captain and led the team up the famous Hampden steps. A few months' gap existed between Boyd's departure after the cup win and the arrival of Rob McKinnon in early 1992 and he helped the club to third and fourth place finishes in the league. Since McKinnon, Stephen McMillan and Stevie Hammell have been popular choices in this most famous of Motherwell positions with the latter earning a Scotland cap and helping the side to third place in 2008.

ON THE MARCH

A lot of what binds football fans together is the sharing of things experienced before and after games; an epic journey to the other end of the country perhaps, or possibly a massive session in the pub after a particularly bad defeat. However, one such sight which will never be forgotten by many Motherwell fans is the march from Stanislas Square in Nancy to the ground before the first leg of the Uefa Cup match in 2008. Between 2,500 and 3,000 fans descended on the French town to see Motherwell's first game in Europe in 14 years and it seemed as though every one of them elected to walk to the ground. The long walk from the centre of the city where fans had been meeting up to drink and sing throughout the day passed through many streets which were full of bemused locals watching the spectacle. There was the wonderful sight of 'Well fans snaking back well over a kilometre en route to the ground where they watched their side battle bravely, but lose 1-0. Graeme Smith's second-half penalty save was the undoubted highlight but despite a bumper crowd of over 11,000 at Fir Park for the return leg, Motherwell were outclassed by the French and eventually lost 3-0 on aggregate. While the result was by no means brilliant, it should be remembered that even as a club below the top level of French football, Nancy's budget stretched to millions and was several times greater than that of Motherwell.

A NOBLE SACRIFICE

It is often remembered that when the club went into administration in 2002, ten players were made redundant while a further nine were released at the first opportunity. However, it should also be remembered that three players, captain Scott Leitch, Derek Adams and Dirk Lehmann, all agreed to stay on at the club but on reduced terms. Cynics may well claim they did this out of self-interest to protect their own positions but occasionally it is more worthy to think the best of people and applaud them for making a sacrifice which helped the club when it was at its lowest ebb. It should also not be forgotten, although frequently is when the media or opposing fans remember our time in administration, that three members of the non-playing staff also lost their jobs.

HAND BAGS IN THE DRESSING ROOM

The circumstances surrounding David Kelly's departure from the club in 2002 have never been openly admitted but they were quite dramatic. After a cup defeat at Dunfermline Athletic he was involved in an altercation with assistant manager Terry Butcher and had his contract cancelled ten days later by mutual consent, although he did play once more.

THE KAISER

Players frequently polarise the opinions of the support but one Fir Park star of modern times that seemed to be universally respected was Martyn Corrigan. The unassuming right-back arrived from Falkirk in 1999 but initially faced stern competition for the right-back spot from Michael Doesburg. Corrigan soon saw off the Dutch player and over the next few years he made the position his own. His calm nature on the ball eventually earned him the nickname of the Kaiser and when the side was filled with kids in the period after administration, he remained a rock of consistency. In 2002/03, Corrigan was on course to have played every minute of every game until he was substituted with half an hour remaining of the season – simply to give superstar James McFadden a reason to take on the captain's armband in what may have been his farewell game. Manager Terry Butcher later admitted to not being aware Corrigan was on the verge of such an accomplishment but thankfully Martyn managed it the following year. Corrigan signed his final deal with Motherwell in 2006 with the intention of completing ten years' service which would have brought a testimonial match; both lucrative to himself and the perfect chance for the fans to thank him for his time at Fir Park. Sadly injuries would take a toll on his performances and when Mark McGhee took charge in 2007 he found his first-team chances limited. It is a measure of the man that rather than choosing to see out a well-paying contract at Fir Park and claim his testimonial, he moved on to Kilmarnock in January 2008 because he wanted to keep playing in the top flight. Alas, injuries continued to dog the Kaiser and his spell at Rugby Park was not overly successful. Motherwell fans will always remember him as both a fine player and true gentleman.

MOTHERWELL IN EUROPE

Motherwell having glory years in the 1930s and 1950s meant that the club missed out on the chance to compete in official European competition when at its strongest. It is one area in which the club is inferior to some others of a similar scale thanks to their best days coming in the 1960s. Hopefully, that is something which will soon be put right! Here is the list of the club's ties in Europe, up to the victory against Flamurtari in the second qualifying round of the Europa League in 2009:

Cup Winners' Cup	1991	GKS Katowice	0-2 (a)	3-1	3-3
UEFA Cup	1994	Havnar Bolteflag	3-0 (h)	4-1	7-1
UEFA Cup	1994	Borussia Dortmund	0-1 (a)	0-2	0-3
UEFA Cup	1995	MyPa 47	1-3 (a)	2-0	3-3
UEFA Cup	2008	Nancy	0-1 (a)	0-2	0-3
Europa League	2009	Llanelli	0-1 (h)	3-0	3-1
Europa League	2009	Flamurtari	0-1 (a)	8-1	8-2

A RARE FEAT

Following the departure of Sieb Dykstra in 1994, Alex McLeish moved quickly to bring in goalkeeping cover. Veteran Ray Allan was signed on a temporary basis and actually featured against Havnar in the away leg. What made this remarkable was that Allan, throughout his long career, never played in the top flight of Scottish football but was eventually given the chance to sample European football at the highest level.

AN OLD BABE

The greatest cup shock in the history of Scottish football came in 1967 when minnows Berwick Rangers defeated Rangers 1-0 at Shielfield Park. Berwick only finished in the middle of the Second Division but they managed to defeat a Rangers side which reached the Cup Winners' Cup Final in Bavaria. Motherwell's claim to fame in this giant-killing is that the goal was scored by Sammy Reid who had been part of the popular Ancell Babes side at Fir Park.

A CAPTAIN'S ROLE

Though the craze for bringing in players from Holland had died down by the middle of the 1990s compared to earlier in the decade, Motherwell were still being boosted by one Dutch player. Mitchell Van Der Gaag was made the club's record signing in 1994 when £400,000 brought him to Fir Park from PSV Eindhoven. His career was stalled after only a couple of games when he picked up a serious injury but when he eventually regained full fitness, he quickly proved to be an asset in the centre of defence. He even chipped in a few goals but ironically every one of them came away from Fir Park until his very last game for the club. With the side trailing Dunfermline Athletic in the final game of 1996/97, a relegation play-off with Airdrie looked certain until captain Van Der Gaag sent a free kick howling into the top corner to rescue a share of the points and spark wild celebrations. He moved back to Holland with FC Utrecht later that summer for £400,000 and the agreement that an autumn friendly would be played between the clubs.

A EURO QUARTET

Only a handful of Scottish players have ever appeared in European competition while playing for four different clubs and two of them achieved the feat with Motherwell. Billy Thompson and Iain Ferguson both played for Motherwell against Katowice in the 1991 Cup Winners' Cup. Thompson also took part with St. Mirren, Dundee United and Rangers while Ferguson's set also included Dundee United and Rangers along with Hearts. Other players to have achieved the feat include Gary Bollan (Rangers, Dundee United, St. Johnstone and Livingston) and Davie Kirkwood (Rangers, Hearts, Airdrie and Raith Rovers).

A PROPER CHRISTENING

New grounds and stands often need to witness momentous events before supporters feel at home in them. The moment of big drama for the Davie Cooper Stand, opened in 1995, came in December 1996 when Ian Ross bundled over a last-minute winner just yards in front of the celebrating fans. The 2-1 win was all the sweeter as Motherwell played for a lot of the second half with midfielder Jamie Dolan in goal following an injury to 'keeper Scott Howie.

TESTING TESTIMONIALS

Originally, Motherwell awarded benefits to players by handing them the profits of lucrative league games, often against the Old Firm, rather than organising separate matches. The likes of George Stevenson and Bobby Ferrier were rewarded in this way but the first friendly match played solely for the benefit of a Fir Park player was against Huddersfield Town, then a leading side in England, in 1929 with Stevenson again being the beneficiary. Since then a number of players have been honoured either as a thank-you for good service or a 'best wishes' gesture after a career has been ended prematurely by injury. Here is a list of post-war Motherwell testimonials:

Charlie Aitken... 1967...Motherwell 1-1 Rangers
Joe Wark.............. 1978.................Motherwell 1-8 West Bromwich Albion
Joe Wark.............. 1985...............................Motherwell 1-3 Old Firm Select
John Gahagan.... 1990.... Motherwell 2-2 Premier League All-Star Select
Colin O'Neill..... 1995................................. Motherwell 3-2 Ipswich Town
Jim Griffin .... 1996..........Motherwell 1-2 Wolverhampton Wanderers
John Philliben.... 1998..........................Motherwell 1-1 West Ham United
Dougie Arnott... 2008...................Motherwell Select 4-5 Old Firm Select

AN UNWANTED RECORD

Motherwell's charge to promotion from the First Division in 1982 produced a high level of optimism for the Scottish Cup that year. A draw pairing Motherwell with Aberdeen, the best side in Scotland at the time, did little to dampen optimism as a large crowd squeezed into Fir Park. It did not last long, though, as a defensive mix-up presented John Hewitt with a golden chance after a mere 9.6 seconds and he made no mistake to claim the quickest recorded goal in the history of the Scottish Cup. Aberdeen, marshalled by a rock-solid defence, had few problems in repelling the limited, if enthusiastic, attack offered by Motherwell and progressed to the next round.

DID YOU KNOW?

Motherwell are the only non-city team to have won every major domestic honour in Scottish football? While Kilmarnock have also won four honours, they have failed to add the League Cup to their trophy cabinet.

A WINNING APPEAL

Celebrations after Motherwell's 9-2 win over Campsie in the Scottish Cup of 1892 were soon put to an end. The opposition successfully managed to appeal the result of the game due to the appalling state of the Dalziel Park pitch. However, the visitors did not fare any better in their second attempt as Motherwell also won that game, albeit by a narrower margin of 6-4.

MOTHERWELL'S MOST REGULAR

Since the Second World War, the following players have made over 300 appearances for the club on league business:

Joe Wark	469
Willie Kilmarnock	452
John Johnston	323
Charlie Aitken	313
Archie Shaw	313
John Philliben	302
Andy Paton	301
Steve Kirk	301

A FAMILY AFFAIR

Motherwell liked to keep it in the family when Billy Davies was manager. He recruited his brother John to strengthen the midfield while John Spencer, signed on loan from Everton and then permanently as Motherwell's record signing, was his brother-in-law. Nepotism is only a fault when things go wrong but sadly John Davies, despite occasionally tidy performances, soon became a target for the supporters who believed his relationship with the boss was what kept him in the team. Spencer was outstanding while on loan but once he agreed a longer-term deal, on astronomical wages, his performances became less consistent. The £600,000 signing ended his Motherwell career with the respectable, if hardly special, record of a goal every four games and joined Colorado in the American Major League as part of a cost cutting exercise. Sadly Spencer and Motherwell were involved in a messy legal dispute over the repayment of a loan several years later.

A CAYMAN DEBACLE

Ged Brannan was one of the gala signings made by Billy Davies shortly after his appointment in autumn 1998 but despite being a player of immense potential, he had a tendency to frustrate the support. Some of his performances – coincidentally when the television cameras were at Fir Park – were superb, and he had a good scoring record. Alternatively, there were times it was felt he did not do enough to justify his large wages and he drew ridicule when he announced he would exploit a passport loophole to play international football for the Cayman Islands. The plucky Islanders planned to fill their team with British players not strong enough to play for their nation of birth but Fifa soon cracked down on the ploy and Brannan was left with egg on his face after just one game, an unofficial international against (Washington) DC United.

ROUND THE BEND

One of the most talented players Motherwell ever signed was the Serbian midfielder, Sasa Curcic. Sadly for Motherwell, by the time Curcic pitched his tent at Fir Park in 2000 his football talents were on the wane and he was becoming known for his lifestyle off the pitch rather than on it. His call at Motherwell, where he only made five appearances, was one of his last before retiring and soon after leaving the club he claimed that millions of pounds could not tempt him to play football again, but the offer of 15 women from around the world would suffice. It is a shame that Curcic's career ended in such comedy fashion as on his day he was an excellent player in the English Premiership, and was capped for Yugoslavia. That said, his eccentricity paid handsomely in a way as he triumphed in the 2008 edition of *Celebrity Big Brother* in his home country.

THE CLAN MCSTAY

Many Scottish clubs have some connection to the McStays, one of the most famous footballing families. While Paul McStay was the most successful, brothers and cousins of his also made a living on the pitch. One of these was cousin John, who moved into the senior ranks with Motherwell and played a handful of games before continuing his career with Clydebank.

HISTORY MADE

After so narrowly failing to overturn the first leg deficit against MyPa 47 in the Uefa Cup in 1995, Motherwell became the first Scottish team to progress after losing at home first in 2009. Whether or not this record is something to be proud of is up for debate as the original 1-0 defeat to Llanelli was one of the worst results in the history of the club. However, once that game had happened the club had to strike back and did so in style in the Welsh town. A couple of thousand fans made the journey down by plane, train and car and were rewarded with a fine performance and 3-0 win thanks to goals from John Sutton (2) and Jamie Murphy as the side progressed to face Flamurtari of Albania in the next round.

A LOAN STAR

One of the best loan signings ever made by the club was Rob Newman in December 1997. Although he only played 11 games for the club either side of Christmas, his experience and physical presence gave the defence a much needed boost in the battle against relegation. Results improved enough to move the team away from the danger of the drop zone and although the club failed in an attempt to keep Newman on a longer basis, he returned to Norwich with the knowledge he had contributed a huge amount to Motherwell in a relatively short space of time.

FLAIR AT EITHER END

Goalkeepers are well known for being eccentric at the best of times and one of the most memorable Motherwell net minders was Keith McCrae. A local lad from Lanark Grammar School, Keith soon proved himself to be a keeper capable of making both tremendous saves and being a substantial presence in the box. His talent was not restricted to in front of his own goal either as he was occasionally pressed into use outfield as a striker, where he also performed well. A big money transfer to Manchester City seemed to have him on the path to fame and fortune but things failed to click for him in England. After moving to Leeds United for a short spell he continued his career in America.

BOSS, YOU'RE DROPPED!

Motherwell manager Billy Davies found himself in the bizarre situation of being able to drop his boss after John Boyle signed Pat Nevin from Kilmarnock to be a player as well as chief executive of the club – the first such combination of roles in Scottish football. Nevin seemed to take his knocks with good grace and actually proved to be a useful player to have for short periods, chipping in with a couple of valuable goals, the most memorable being a fantastic winner deep into injury time against Hearts at home. Nevin contributed on the pitch for a couple of years before retiring to focus on the business side of the game but sadly his performance in the boardroom was not nearly so impressive and the club plunged into administration under his watch in 2002.

BARREN RUNS

There is often a belief in football that one team will hold an Indian sign over another or that one particular ground is unlucky. In Motherwell's case, there are two long stretches which instantly spring to mind. One is at Tannadice Park where Motherwell failed to beat Dundee United in 32 attempts between January 1976 and February 1994. Typically enough, the streak was finally broken with the aid of the hosts who scored all three goals – two into their own net – in a 2-1 win for the Steelmen. The other is at Pittodrie, home of Aberdeen. When goals from Rob McKinnon, Steve Kirk and Tommy Coyne gave the Steelmen a 3-1 victory in the Granite City in October 1994, it ended a run of 38 league games at Pittodrie without a win, the last coming in April 1966. However, Motherwell did win twice at Pittodrie in the 28-year gap between league wins when Bobby Graham's goal produced a Scottish Cup quarter-final win in 1975 and Steve Kirk's solitary strike in 1991 kicked off the run which resulted in the cup being lifted at Hampden Park later in the year. Alarmingly, the next such run is already forming although perhaps it is not so surprising that it is at the home of one half of the Old Firm. Since an Owen Coyle double gave Motherwell a crucial bank holiday win at Ibrox in May 1997, the team have failed to win in their next 22 visits on league business.

PAT NEVIN WAS BOTH PLAYER AND CHIEF EXECUTIVE IN HIS TIME AT FIR PARK.

CRUSHED AT HAMPDEN (1)

Motherwell's side of 1975 seemed to be heading for glory when a run to Hampden in the Scottish Cup threw up a local semi-final against rivals Airdrie. Things were going well when Willie Pettigrew gave the Steelmen the lead but the Diamonds did not give up without a fight. An own goal from Stewart McLaren was enough to give them a replay they barely deserved and they continued their luck in the second match. The tie was evenly poised when the referee penalised goalkeeper Stuart Rennie for taking more than the four steps allowed with the ball in his hands. This was a very rare infringement to give, but Airdrie made the most of their good fortune by scrambling home the only goal from the indirect free kick. At least Motherwell could take some consolation from the fact Airdrie would lose the final 3-1 to Celtic.

CRUSHED AT HAMPDEN (2)

Just a year later, Motherwell found themselves back at Hampden and facing Rangers in another Scottish Cup semi-final. Once more things looked to be going swimmingly when goals from Pettigrew and McLaren seemed to have the team on the verge of a first major cup final in 22 years. Unfortunately, the fates conspired again and a soft penalty won by Derek Johnstone allowed Rangers back into the match. A good penalty claim at the other end was turned down and Rangers completed their comeback to win 3-2 and deny the Steelmen yet again. Rangers won the final against Hearts 3-1, famously scoring their first goal before the official starting time of three o'clock as the referee began proceedings early.

THE SECOND MCFADYEN

Motherwell fans frequently bemoan the lack of a striker with Willie McFadyen's legendary capabilities in front of goal but supporters in the 1950s were actually able to watch a second McFadyen. His son Ian was signed from Dundee United by Bobby Ancell but the versatile player failed to make the same impact at Fir Park as his father (perhaps not surprisingly!) and left after making only 25 league appearances. He was no slouch on the football field, though, and contributed to Dundee United's promotion to the top flight later in his career.

ON THE SPOT

One of the most prolific Fir Park strikers of the post-war years was Dixie Deans. He was signed for a mere £100 to replace another famous forward, Joe McBride, who had moved on to Celtic. Deans was the classic bustling front man who found both the net, and trouble, with disciplinary problems blighting his time at Fir Park. He had already been sent off several times before Jock Stein finally managed to take him to Celtic in a deal worth only £17,500 in a bid to give the player a much needed fresh start. However, any annoyance the Motherwell fans had at their star player moving for such a paltry sum was negated considerably by him blazing a crucial first penalty over the bar in the 1972 European Cup semi-final shoot-out at Celtic Park which Inter Milan would go on to win 5-4.

A THREE-MENDOUS TREBLE

When Ancell Babe Pat Delaney broke into the side he made his debut in defence but when moved into the attack a couple of seasons later he showed remarkable skill to grab three league hat-tricks in just eight weeks. He also scored a pair of goals in the Summer Cup win of 1965 but instead it was generally believed that defence was probably his best position after all: what the club would do now to have the strength in depth that such a scorer could be used at the back!

THIS IS OUR HOUSE

Motherwell's glory years at the start of the 1930s were largely based on sensational home form. Between losing at home to Hearts in September 1929 and to Partick Thistle in October 1932, the club played 59 league matches at Fir Park without tasting defeat. After the Hearts loss, 18 ties were won in succession before Kilmarnock managed to take a draw, although the run did lose some of its gloss thanks to Rangers not only winning a Scottish Cup tie at Fir Park but scoring five goals in the process. Kilmarnock deserve credit for being particularly resolute opponents as they were the only side who left Fir Park, in both the league and cup, without being defeated in Motherwell's championship season of 1931/32.

A COSTLY KICK

Gary McAllister stepped up to take one of the most crucial kicks in Scottish football history when Scotland were awarded a penalty against England in Euro 96. Sadly for Gary, and the nation, he blasted his shot straight at Seaman who made the save. Motherwell fans would have felt particular sympathy for Gary, a local lad and 'Well fan, who came through the youth ranks at Fir Park to become a key member of the 1984/85 side which won the First Division. Financial troubles meant Gary was sold to Leicester City in a deal including Ally Mauchlen and over the next two decades he thrived in England, winning the league title with Leeds United, the FA Cup, League Cup and Uefa Cup with Liverpool along with collecting 57 international caps for Scotland, and an MBE.

VIENNESE WALTZ

In the summer of 1997, Motherwell made a huge fanfare of two high profile signings. Striker Mario Dorner and full-back Franz Resch had both been recruited from Austrian club VfL Modling on free transfers under the Bosman ruling. The expected boost in morale and season ticket sales duly happened before it later emerged the club had only signed the pair on very short-term contracts. Not only that, Modling were also disputing whether or not Motherwell had the right to sign them in the first place! As often happens, the hype was much greater than the reality and though the two players could have done a job, Resch in particular, they were quietly released to try their luck in England a couple of months later.

FINDING THE RANGE

Motherwell's modern-day record against Rangers is nothing to be proud of but there was one glorious season when Rangers belonged firmly on the Fir Park mantlepiece. In 1959/60 the clubs met in the group stages of the League Cup with Motherwell winning each game home and away 2-1. The run of form continued in the league with another Fir Park victory, again by 2-1, before the quadruple was completed at Ibrox late in the year with a 2-0 win.

THE SCORING CHART

Here is Motherwell's top-ten league scorers since World War Two:

Player	Goals	Apps
Pat Quinn	83	196
Ian St. John	80	113
Willie Pettigrew	80	166
Dixie Deans	78	152
Wilson Humphries	69	199
Archie Kelly	66	104
Jimmy Watson	66	195
Steve Kirk	63	301
Tommy Coyne	59	132
Dougie Arnott	59	240

EARLY BIRDS

Motherwell's July 2nd match against Llanelli was by far the earliest the club has ever started a competitive campaign. With the league season traditionally starting in August, fans had to deal with quite a shock in 2009 although they were given a taste by previous SPL seasons which started on the last weekend in July. The earliest of these was season 2001/02 which opened on July 28th, although sadly Motherwell still seemed to be on their summer holidays when they lost 5-2 at Dunfermline Athletic on that day. Billy Davies played a very lightweight midfield which while technically strong, lacked the physical strength needed to compete and despite a penalty from debutant David Kelly, the side were swept away by four goals in the second half.

MISSING THE BOAT

Motherwell were beaten 5-0 by a Brazil Select on their last match of the 1928 tour of South America but given the heavy nature of the defeat, they can be grateful that they had an obvious excuse to hand. The team had so little time to catch the boat home after the game that they rushed to the port still dressed in their playing clothes so it is little surprise their minds were elsewhere! The complete tour consisted of eleven matches of which Motherwell won six, lost four and drew one.

SEVENTH HEAVEN

Cup ties against lower league opposition at Fir Park frequently seem to fill Motherwell fans with dread. Perhaps it is the rare feeling of heavy expectation which causes the problem but nervous fans often lead to nervous players, and that leads to disasters. While a home defeat against Queen's Park many years ago will forever haunt the memory – and losses to the likes of Ayr United and Dundee provide more recent scars – one pleasant exception to the rule that these games are inevitably tricky came in 1990. While Clyde were not performing wonderfully in the First Division it was expected that they would put up some resistance in the Scottish Cup at Fir Park. Instead, the Motherwell fans were treated to an exhibition of football as the side romped to a convincing 7-0 win with seven separate scorers inflicting misery on the small band of travelling Clyde fans. Chris McCart, Davie Cooper, Steve Kirk, Dougie Arnott, John Gahagan, Bobby Russell and Stevie Bryce all finished on the scoresheet.

THE SHED'S LAST STAND

For many years the vociferous section of the Motherwell support used to gather near the segregation fence in the middle of the covered enclosure. This was where anyone wanting to make an impact on the atmosphere would stand. The away fans were conveniently located just a few yards away which inspired the banter. The Shed, as it became affectionately known, if not particularly uniquely, saw many great games which produced some famous victories and heartbreaking defeats. Alas, it was condemned forever when the Taylor Report demanded that seating be made compulsory at football grounds and from season 1991/92 plastic seats would be bolted on to the terracing. Thankfully, the Shed and those who stood in it for so long, were able to wave it off into the history books in appropriate fashion with a 3-0 hammering of Rangers in the penultimate game of 1990/91. John Philliben opened the scoring before a late double from Dougie Arnott, after a penalty had been blazed onto the north terracing by Mark Walters, put Motherwell in dreamland and effectively offered the championship on a plate to Aberdeen. The second and third goals meant the Dons only needed a draw at Ibrox to win the league on the last day but instead their bottle crashed and Rangers scraped home again.

THE EAST STAND REPLACED THE COVERED ENCLOSURE AT FIR PARK.

THE ALBANIA TEN

If those who made the arduous journey to Poland in 1991 to watch the club's first ever game in European competition are admired, the ten bold fans who made the journey to Albania in 2009 deserve similar recognition. The short gap between defeating Llanelli in the first Europa League qualifying round and travelling to Flamurtari for the next round was problematic and it is fair to say the club did not help matters by discouraging fans from travelling. Nevertheless, ten supporters decided to make the long journey anyway and they were rewarded with a battling performance, albeit one which ended in a controversial defeat. The referee appeared to make an error in interpreting the rules for encroachment at a penalty kick when he demanded John Sutton re-take his successful strike which he duly missed second time around. Flamurtari were boosted by this and emerged 1-0 winners going into the second leg to be played in Scotland. Thankfully Motherwell came through in sensational fashion to win 8-2 on aggregate – but with the half-time score standing at 6-0, no doubt the Albania ten were soon making plans to get to Bucharest for the next round!

A DEADLY DUO (2)

Throughout the early to mid-1980s, Motherwell fans could have been forgiven for resting on their crush barriers and dreaming of the relatively glory days of Bobby Graham and Willie Pettigrew from years before. Though the side did score plenty of goals in 1981/82, that was in the First Division and it is fair to say that the next truly great striking partnership at the club was only formed in late 1993. Dougie Arnott had already been at Fir Park for a number of years, and had eventually excelled after a slow start, but it was the arrival of Tommy Coyne which gave him a truly worthy partner. Coyne was keen to return to Scotland after unfortunate personal circumstances ruined his spell at Tranmere Rovers and Tommy McLean persuaded him to come to Motherwell instead of Kilmarnock. That proved to be a magnificent decision as Coyne and Arnott hit off a superb partnership as Motherwell finished third and second in consecutive seasons. Arnott's work-rate, combined with Coyne's vision and movement, created the perfect partnership and with both being deadly in front of goal, there were no problems in finishing either.

HAVE A MERRY CHRISTMAS!

Unlike in England, the big Scottish time for football in the festive season is – or at least was – Ne'er Day rather than Christmas Day but Motherwell have still played some matches when the non-footballing world was content to eat turkey and open presents. Between 1897 and 1971 Motherwell took to the field 11 times on Christmas Day with the first match being a draw at home to Hamilton and the last a similar result at East Fife. In between the club faced Morton, Dumbarton, Ayr United, Queen's Park, Partick Thistle, Queen of the South, East Fife, Falkirk and Dundee and has a record of five wins, three draws and three defeats from matches played on Christmas Day.

EURO GOALS

Motherwell's scorers in European competition, up to and including the match against Flamurtari:

5... Steve Kirk
4...Jamie Murphy
2...........Alex Burns, John Sutton, Ross Forbes

Nick Cusack, Tommy Coyne, Paul McGrillen, Billy Davies, Shaun McSkimming, Dougie Arnott, Paul Slane, Shaun Hutchison and Robert McHugh have all scored one goal each.

THE BIGGEST CROWD IN YEARS

When Motherwell won the cup in 1991 fans who had been at Hampden to watch the final, and those who stayed behind in the town, immediately rushed to Fir Park to start the celebrations. The side eventually made it back from Glasgow where they took to the Main Stand at Fir Park to show the cup to the thousands of fans who were waiting on the pitch below, as well as in the terraces surrounding the ground. The large turnout prompted cup hero Steve Kirk, who scored in every round of the competition including the winner in the final, to remark that ground had witnessed the "biggest crowd in years" when there was not even a game to be seen! Despite the cup final success the regular attendance at Fir Park did not really increase and was not helped by the following season, 1991/92, being something of an anti-climax.

THE MAN WHO MADE MOTHERWELL

In a club with a history of inspiring and famous individuals, there is one who stands out above all the rest. However, should a visitor arrive at Fir Park for a match, or just a visit, it would be almost impossible to find a trace of the great man – John 'Sailor' Hunter. Although the club had managed to become established in the First Division in the years before his appointment in 1911, success appeared a forlorn hope as the side had not even managed to finish in the top half of the table. Hunter was selected as the man to help the club progress at a meeting of the directors held in the Commercial Hotel in Hamilton following a defeat against the local rivals. Having earned a Scottish cap and a Scottish Cup winners' medal while at Dundee, Hunter was seeing out his playing career at Clyde when approached by Motherwell to become manager. He made a slow start finishing 14th in his first season, and it was only after the First World War that he began to make progress – even if he did sign future legends Hugh Ferguson and Bobby Ferrier when hostilities were still under way. The team finished third in 1920 but slipped back down the table in future years. Hunter began to get things right on a consistent basis from 1927 when the club finished as runners-up, and then remained in the top three of Scottish football for a further seven seasons. While the Scottish Cup proved elusive thanks to three cup final defeats in the 1930s, the championship was collected by five points in 1932, making Motherwell the only team outside of the Old Firm to win the title between the wars. Hunter had moulded the side into one of the finest ever seen with stars such as George Stevenson and Willie McFadyen joining Ferrier in becoming both dedicated and skilful servants. Hunter, though responsible to the Board of directors, was also club secretary which effectively gave him complete control in the running of the club. He resigned as team manager after the war, suggesting George Stevenson to be his successor, but continued as secretary until 1959 when he was forced to retire due to ill health at the age of 80. Hunter's association with the club spanned an astonishing 48 years, a period which saw the side turn from being perennial strugglers in the top flight to champions of Scotland, along with collecting both domestic cups.

THE YOUNGEST EVER – MAYBE!

Motherwell's lack of exact record-keeping before the war means that some bits of trivia which are commonly known for other clubs are not so clear. It is generally thought that the youngest player to take to the field in claret and amber, in the league at least, was 16-year-old Tommy Coakley in 1964. Sadly, his career at Fir Park did not turn out to be a great success and he moved on to Leicester City a couple of years after making his debut. Tommy's uncle, also called Tommy, was reported to be interested in buying the club from John Boyle in 2007 but a deal could not be agreed.

BECOMING PROFESSIONALS

While money may be sloshing around the highest level of football today, the issue of cash was not always so clear cut. Towards the end of the 19th century amateurism was still believed to be the way forward with then Glasgow giants Queen's Park dominating football north of the border. However, it soon became clear that English clubs were easily able to tempt away the best Scottish footballers with offers of gold, and eventually the decision was made to allow open professionalism in Scotland. The Motherwell Board met for the AGM in 1893 to discuss whether or not the club would follow suit and it was agreed to do so. The first game as professionals brought instant success with a 4-1 win over local rivals Hamilton Academical but the decision, given how the game went, was clearly the right one. Queen's Park, despite their ten Scottish Cup wins, are now stuck in the lower leagues, notable only for their amateur status in a world which has otherwise left them behind.

EVERYBODY OUT

During the Second World War, advice was given to spectators that in the event of an air-bombing raid they should take shelter at the ground rather than rushing home. Remarkably, 40 years later, exploding devices were cause for concern again when a bomb threat was phoned in to the Vice Presidents' Club during a game against Hearts in 1985. The police evacuated the covered terracing as they searched for the device but none was found and the game continued with Motherwell winning 2-1.

INTERNATIONAL STARS

For many years the most capped Motherwell player was George Stevenson before Tommy Coyne and Simo Valikari managed to edge ahead of him. However, both of those players have now been considerably outstripped by Northern Ireland star Stephen Craigan. Craigs actually picked up his first couple of caps while at Partick Thistle but it was only after his return to Motherwell that he sealed a regular place in the squad. Since re-signing in 2003, he has been capped 38 times by Northern Ireland, taking his total appearances to 40. Perhaps unsurprisingly, given that his club career has yielded only seven goals in nearly 400 matches, he has yet to find the net for his country but he has been involved in sensational victories over Spain, England and Sweden. Craigan has become one of the most respected players at Fir Park and through his two spells at the club he has racked up around 250 games. Following the departure of Mark McGhee in the summer of 2009, it was Craigan who was asked to take over as caretaker manager until a replacement could be found. He has also moved into the media, working as an analyst for the BBC.

SCOTLAND CAPS

Here is the list of the most capped Scottish players while at Fir Park. It is unlikely the top of the table will change much in years to come as now any player in the national squad so often is likely to be sold very quickly!

Player	Caps	Time period
George Stevenson	12	1928-1935
Willie Redpath	9	1949-1952
Ian St. John	7	1959-1961
Andy Weir	6	1959-1960
Bert McCann	5	1959-1961
Willie Pettigrew	5	1976-1977
Pat Quinn	4	1961-1962
Tom Boyd	4	1991
James McFadden	4	2002-2003

STEPHEN CRAIGAN IS MOTHERWELL'S MOST CAPPED PLAYER BY QUITE SOME DISTANCE.

THE NAME ON THE SHIRT

Motherwell's first sponsorship deal was with Scottish Brewers in the 1980s but the practice only became established a few years later through local car dealer Ian Skelly. A long lasting relationship formed between the club and the business and when Motherwell lifted the Scottish Cup in 1991 it was the Skelly name which was worn on the shirts. After the end of that season Motorola moved to fill the gap with the international company pointing out that their Lanarkshire plant gave them a substantial local interest. That partnership lasted for 11 seasons but ended at the worst possible time as the club sunk into administration. Once more a local firm stepped into the breach with The Untouchables taking over but the era of long associations with one firm was well and truly over. Here is a list of sponsors since that fateful 2002-03 campaign:

2002-2004............................The Untouchables
2004-2006................................Zoom Airlines
2006-2008...............................Anglian Homes
2008-present..JAXX

WHEN ONE DEFEAT IS NOT ENOUGH

The chaotic leagues which took place in the First World War often gave sides little respite for recovery between matches. On one occasion in April 1916, Motherwell actually played Ayr United and Celtic on the same day and contrived to lose both games! Sadly there was no excuse of tiredness to be offered as Celtic also played twice on the same day but they were rather more successful, beating Raith Rovers along with Motherwell. The day was notable for being the debut of Jock Rundell who would go on to excel in goal, making 270 appearances in Sailor Hunter's side which was setting out on the path to glory.

DID YOU KNOW?

Willie McFadyen scored four goals in the opening league game of the championship season and then found the net at such a rate his strike average never dropped below a goal per game for the entire year! He finished with 52 goals from 34 appearances, an average higher than 1.5 per match.

WHAT MIGHT HAVE BEEN

Motherwell only managed to secure Premier League football on the penultimate day of the season in 1992/93 but the next year would be spent at the other end of the table. The club made an excellent opening with a draw against Celtic being followed by wins over Dundee, Kilmarnock and Raith Rovers that quickly put the side top of the league. Though there were occasionally frustrating defeats, in general the team swept all before them with the likes of Paul Lambert, Phil O'Donnell and Tommy Coyne all making massive contributions going forward. Defensively, Sieb Dykstra in goal was supported by the excellent Brian Martin and Miodrag Krivocapic and as spring approached the side were still in the midst of a genuine title challenge – the first in nearly 40 years. A harsh defeat at Rangers, thanks to a deflection and a penalty, left the club with an uphill task but when the team defeated the same opposition at Fir Park the race was kept alive for a few more weeks. Sadly Motherwell stumbled in their closing games and took only one point from the last six available. Had all three of the final matches been won, the league table shows Motherwell would have been champions by a point – a fact which really puts a 'what if' feeling on a season which was superb and brought European football through a third-place finish. In reality, the support has little to regret as Rangers took their foot off the gas in the closing games with the championship secured. Surely they would have taken more than one point from relegation strugglers Kilmarnock and Dundee if they had to... or so we would like to believe! The side, under the guidance of Alex McLeish, actually went one better to finish second in 1994/95, well behind champions Rangers, and failed to sustain a real title challenge.

OUT THE DOOR

Motherwell were forced to make a number of players redundant on entering administration in 2002, but one player had been kicked out of the club years before. Colin McNair was a squad player when he assaulted teammate Jim Griffin at training in 1989 and was promptly sacked by manager Tommy McLean. McNair had only made a couple of appearances for Motherwell and failed to make the most of a second chance offered by Falkirk.

NAMES FROM THE NETHERLANDS

Motherwell's links with Holland have been strong for some time and even though none of the current squad are Dutch, many players from that famous footballing nation have graced Fir Park. However, looking through the list there is no doubt some were a greater success than others! Some failed to settle, or were hampered by injury, but Luc Nijholt played in the cup-winning team and Sieb Dykstra helped the side to third place in the league in his final season. And, of course, Mitchell Van Der Gaag saved the side from a relegation play-off with Airdrie with almost his last kick for the club.

Player	Time
Luc Nijholt	1990-1993
Bart Verheul	1991-1992
Rob Maaskant	1991-1992
Sieb Dykstra	1991-1994
Elroy Kromheer	1992-1993
Mitchell Van Der Gaag	1994-1997
Jan Michels	1998-1999
Rob Matthei	1998-2000
Michael Doesburg	1998-2000

YOUNG LADIES (NOT) ON DISPLAY

The sight of cheerleaders at games is often viewed as being both a tacky and recent phenomenon but had the Motherwell Board decided differently, they could have been a fixture at Fir Park for some years. In 1954 the Butlins' Young Lady Display Team wrote to the club to offer their services but the conservative suits in the Fir Park boardroom declined to take them up. It was probably for the best!

THE MORE THINGS CHANGE

After Motherwell won the cup in 1991, it was an optimistic crowd who travelled to Raith Rovers for the first competitive match of the next season. However, far from continuing in cup-winning form, the fans discovered Motherwell had reverted to type and Raith won the League Cup tie 4-1.

THE RETURN OF THE CONDEMNED MAN

One of Tommy McLean's most controversial signings was Neil Simpson, who arrived at the club in 1991. Simpson had been an important part of the all-conquering Aberdeen side of the 1980s but was vilified for a tackle on Ian Durrant which resulted in the Rangers player being out injured for a couple of years. Simpson performed well during his short time at Fir Park and chipped in a vital goal in a victory against Airdrie. One of his best performances was in a cup defeat at Ibrox, despite being abused for the whole game by the home fans, and he eventually tired of being consistently placed under a media spotlight. He left to return to a more secluded career in the Highland League.

THE 'WELL ON THE WEB

As Motherwell fans took their first stumbling steps through the new world of the internet, many would have been delighted to find a presence online devoted to the club. James Reid's Unofficial Motherwell Homepage was a great source of news for fans home and abroad for many years following its inception in 1995 and has since been joined by other sites including FirParkCorner.com and Steelmenonline.co.uk. After being slow to adapt to the necessity of having a strong website, Motherwellfc.co.uk also made a dramatic improvement over the years.

DAILY DERBY

The demands of television now means fans are accustomed to games being played on every day of the week, but it was not always so with Saturday being the holy day for football supporters up and down the country. However, the desire to play games on public holidays such as Ne'er Day did mean Motherwell first played on a Monday against St. Mirren in 1905, and on a Friday against Airdrie in 1909. The first Sunday game did not take place for several more decades when Brechin City were defeated in the cup in 1974. While fans may still turn out at odd days and times, the vast majority would prefer to keep their football where they think it belongs – Saturday at three o'clock.

ON A HOT STREAK

In contrast to times when goals would prove hard to come by from the whole team, there were occasional instances of some players simply being unable to do anything other than score. The longest scoring streak in the league came in 1937 and belongs to Duncan Ogilvie – unless stated otherwise, he scored once per game:

Motherwell 2-1 Aberdeen (Ogilvie 2)
Kilmarnock 0-2 Motherwell
Motherwell 3-3 Hearts
Queen's Park 1-3 Motherwell
Motherwell 4-1 Morton (Ogilvie 2)
Motherwell 3-2 Falkirk
Hibs 1-1 Motherwell
Dundee 2-2 Motherwell
Motherwell 3-2 St. Mirren (Ogilvie 2)

BLOWING COLD

The team could definitely have done with a modern-day Duncan Ogilvie in 1995-96 when they managed to go eight games without scoring across the turn of the year. Indeed, the match that snapped the run, a 1-0 win at Brockville, could also be included as those points were actually provided by a Joe McLaughlin own goal. When incorporating games before the run started, Motherwell managed to play 15 matches and find the net only twice of their own accord. Both goals came from Alex Burns but the desperate fans, who witnessed a mere three goals in 22.5 hours of football, must have wondered why they bothered. Motherwell finished the season with a miserly 28 goals from 36 games but eventually survived comfortably in the league, mainly thanks to an impressive defence which only conceded 39; by far and away the best total outside of the Old Firm.

DID YOU KNOW?

The only Motherwell player to miss penalty kicks in two shoot-outs is John Philliben. He failed from the spot against Celtic in 1986 and Alloa in 1996, both times in the League Cup.

ALEX BURNS WAS A RARE MOTHERWELL GOALSCORER IN SEASON 1995/96.

A PAINFULLY SLOW START

While Tommy McLean is rightfully remembered as one of the best managers in the history of the club, it should also be noted that some seasons were distinctly grim. In 1988/89 it took an astonishing 17 attempts before Motherwell managed to win a match in the league although there was at least some small consolation in the form of a League Cup win over Airdrie in the meantime. Eventually, Hearts were beaten 2-0 at Fir Park and despite the poor start, the woeful performance of Hamilton Academical over the entire campaign ensured Motherwell survived in the Premier League. The failures in the first 16 games were as follows:

Hibs (a) 0-1
Dundee (h) 1-1
Hamilton (a) 0-1
Rangers (h) 0-2
St. Mirren (a) 0-1
Dundee United (h).......................................1-2
Celtic (a)...1-3
Aberdeen (h) 1-1
Hearts (a) 2-2
Dundee (a) 1-1
Hibs (h) 1-1
Dundee United (a) 1-1
St. Mirren (h)..1-2
Rangers (a) 1-2
Hamilton (h)..1-1
Aberdeen (a) 1-2

QUICK SHOT ST. JOHN

For many years, the record of the quickest hat-trick in British senior football was held by a Motherwell player. Ian St. John slammed in three goals in a remarkable 150 seconds to secure a 3-1 win at Hibs in a 1959 League Cup tie as Motherwell went on to top their group. Sadly, the side lost heavily in the two-legged quarter-final against Hearts.

THE PERFECT START

On the other hand, the start made by the team in 1933 would surely have convinced many fans that another title would be on its way to Fir Park. The first four games were won without conceding a goal and though Rangers found the net in the fifth match, the winning run continued. Nine games were won in succession before Aberdeen managed a draw, but that was only a minor blip. The next 12 contests passed without defeat with only two draws representing dropped points. The team eventually lost for the first time to Clyde, just two days before Christmas, but inconsistency late in the season saw the team miss out on the championship. In fairness to the players, their total of 62 points would more often than not have been enough but they were undone by a magnificent effort by Rangers. The opening nine victories were:

Clyde (a)..	1-0
St. Johnstone (h)	1-0
Dundee (h)	1-0
Queen of the South (a)	5-0
Rangers (h)	2-1
Hamilton (a)	2-1
Hibs (a)	2-0
Aberdeen (h)...	4-1
Queen's Park (a)...	5-1

A HAT-TRICK OF HAT-TRICKS

No Motherwell player has ever managed to notch three hat-tricks in successive league games despite several prodigious feats of scoring, especially in the 1920s and 1930s. The closest anyone came to this was Hugh Ferguson in 1920 when he scored nine in three games but did not quite manage the correct distribution. He grabbed four of the goals in the 6-0 rout of Queen's Park, and three in a 4-2 victory over Falkirk, but fell short by only managing a brace in the 2-1 win against St. Mirren, which came in between. Just over ten years later, Willie McFadyen also went close but could only score a double after consecutive hat-tricks in early 1931.

OPTIMISM 20 YEARS TOO SOON

The development of floodlights at Fir Park took several stages and in 1972 the Board requested a quote for the cost of upgrading the lighting to the level required by Uefa to host continental games. Alas, that turned out to be somewhat ambitious as despite a couple of cup semi-finals, and a fourth-place league finish in the decade, European football would not be achieved until winning the Scottish Cup in 1991, nearly 20 years later.

A SECOND RELEGATION...

After the bonus of not being relegated despite finishing second from bottom in 1955, Motherwell managed to stabilise themselves as a top flight side for several years. A couple of mid-table finishes and the excitement of the Ancell era was to follow but, as with all provincial clubs, good things would inevitably come to an end. Under Bobby Howitt, the club failed to match the performances under Ancell and this reached a zenith in 1967/68 when the club were relegated for the second time in history. A disastrous start saw only one victory collected in the first 16 games, and although there was a marked improvement over the Christmas period there was no doubt that the team was in deep trouble. A return to the form of the earlier part of the season produced an equally mediocre two wins from the final 14 matches and the team eventually finished second from bottom, six points adrift of Raith Rovers.

...BUT SOON A SECOND PROMOTION

Manager Howitt kept his job as the side dropped into the Second Division and was put under pressure by a disappointing League Cup campaign. Significant players such as Joe Wark, Jumbo Muir and Tom Forsyth were all brought into the side and their impact was immediate. The team quickly moved to the top of the table, seemingly scoring goals at will, and though there were occasional defeats, no one else in the league could consistently match the Steelmen. Promotion was sealed in April with a win at Boghead and a week later the championship was secured with a hammering of Stenhousemuir. Motherwell's much needed return to the highest division of Scottish football had been successfully secured at the first time of asking.

A QUESTION OF HYGIENE

Football stadiums were not always the modern and safe venues we know today. Many people think back to a golden era when the slopes of Fir Park terracing were still literally in existence and not just a line in a song. The old days had definite drawbacks as well. In 1970, an inspector from the Burgh Sanitary Department was forced to write to the club demanding action be taken over the number of beer cans being stored behind the terracing. The club were requested to either remove them or at least cover them up during the close season. One, no doubt suitably sheepish, director volunteered to look into the task.

THINGS GOING FROM BAD TO WORSE

Flamurtari have every reason to feel hard done by in their heavy defeat to Motherwell in the 2009/10 Europa League. Not only were they well beaten, but improvements being made to the Fir Park playing surface meant the tie was played in Airdrie at New Broomfield. The Motherwell fans soon started taking pity on their Albanian counterparts as the diary section of the *Herald* newspaper reported that one wag, observing the glum travelling support, remarked to his companion: "And all they have to look forward to now is a night out in Airdrie!" Rumours that the Albanians brought packages of food and clothing for Airdrie residents remain unsubstantiated.

A LACK OF TRUST

In the aftermath of Motherwell going into administration in 2002, the fans quickly formed a group to help raise money to aid the survival of the club. From there, the Motherwell Supporters Trust was formed with the goal of buying shares in the club to give the fans a voice at Board level. Sadly, it quickly became apparent that as John Boyle owned such a huge stake in the club, gaining enough shares to earn serious representation would not be possible. The Trust arguably lost sight of its goals and though it continued to organise events and raise money for the club's youth teams and physiotherapy room, it seemed to lack a raison d'être. In summer 2009 the Trust was struggling to find members to fill the positions on its Board and faced an uncertain future.

THERE'S NO SUCH THING AS A FREE LUNCH

Even before the harsh lessons of administration, Motherwell were eager to cut back on expenses whenever possible. In 1964 the Board decided that the average price of 9/- per player for lunch in Robb's restaurant was too high and this should be limited by Mr Robb to only five or six shillings. Manager Bobby Ancell was given the delicate task of breaking the news to the players that they would have to cut back on their eating habits.

IN FULL COLOUR

Motherwell moved to capitalise on the expected big crowd for the Texaco Cup return leg with Tottenham Hotspur in 1970 by improving the match programme, the *Fir Park News*. The issue was the first by the club to be published using colour, rather than just black and white printing, and the size was also extended with additional articles being included. Fans were asked to stump up an extra shilling for the edition but those who did had a memorable souvenir as Motherwell romped home 3-1 to progress 5-4 on aggregate.

YOUNG GUNS GO FOR IT

Motherwell's youth policy has produced a number of players who claimed international honours for Scotland at levels below the full international team. While most manage a handful of caps for the under-21 side before graduating to the big eleven, or becoming overage, one player stands out with many more appearances than anyone else. Lee McCulloch played 14 times for the young Scots with the second most capped player for Motherwell at this level being Phil O'Donnell, who managed eight.

FANTASTIC FOUR

The last Motherwell player to go on a scoring spree in one game by getting more than three goals in 90 minutes was Steve Kirk in 1990. Despite several players notching hat-tricks in either league or cup competitions, no one has managed to repeat the feat of Kirk's four goals against St. Mirren at the end of season 1989/90. Remarkably, all four of his strikes in a 4-0 win came courtesy of his right foot, although he was equally competent with his left and head.

STEVE KIRK SCORED FOUR IN A GAME IN 1990 BUT THERE WAS EVEN BETTER TO COME THE FOLLOWING YEAR. . .

A LEGEND OFF THE PITCH

One of the many legends of Fir Park was, for many years, responsible for the upkeep of the pitch rather than just playing on it. Groundsman Andy Russell had been in charge of guarding the grass for the better part of 40 years when he retired in 1994. Sadly he was soon struck by illness and died a couple of years later. Russell, along with dog Tizer, was ferocious in protecting his pitch from unwelcome intruders during the week and it is quite possible that if he could have his way, players would not have been permitted to use it even on Saturdays! He saw many good sides during his time at Fir Park but one of the most memorable sights of the 1991 cup triumph was Andy puffing away on a huge cigar during the open-topped bus ride through the town. Though maintaining the pitch was different in his day, due to the terraces at either end of the pitch allowing plenty of sunlight, it is highly questionable as to whether Andy would have allowed 'his' pitch to deteriorate to the extent it did before major repair work was undertaken in the summer of 2009.

SEMI-FINAL DAY

Scottish Cup semi-finals are usually played around the same time of year but fate dealt Motherwell a particularly interesting hand on one certain day. No fewer than five cup semi-finals have been played by the club on March 31st but in general the day should be forgotten as only one contest turned out to be successful with the other four ending in defeats. And even the victory over Hibs only led to a final loss against Celtic. If further proof were needed about the curse on this day, it arrived in 1984 when Motherwell's relegation to the First Division was confirmed with a loss at Rangers. The semi-final record reads:

1934......................Motherwell 1-3 St. Mirren
1951..............................Motherwell 3-2 Hibs
1962..........................Motherwell 1-3 Rangers
1965................Motherwell 0-3 Celtic (replay)
1976..........................Motherwell 2-3 Rangers

THE FIRST LANARKSHIRE UNITED

When newspapers broke the story – which was promptly denied – of Motherwell chairman John Boyle trying to create a Lanarkshire super club through merging the four local teams, the fans responded with outrage. However, this was far from being the first consideration of abolishing local sides in Motherwell, Airdrie, Hamilton and Coatbridge for the greater good as the idea was actually mooted in December 1972. Director Angus Hepburn brought up discussion of the possibility at a Motherwell Board meeting, but the idea did not progress. A Lanarkshire United finally came into existence 30 years later but it was a girls' club which put out teams at various age levels from under-17 downwards. In 2008, Motherwell officially brought the sides into the club and they have continued to enjoy successes by collecting trophies at a variety of different age groups.

THE HEAVIEST DEFEAT

Motherwell's dismal campaign in 1978/79 was doomed to end in failure and relegation but there was to be further ignominy heaped upon the club. In the middle of an 11-game losing streak, the side travelled to Aberdeen on a Monday evening and were duly hammered 8-0. This broke a record which had stood for some 78 years to become the biggest-ever loss suffered by a Motherwell side, and retains its place in the history books to this day. Motherwell have never conceded nine or more in a competitive game and there have only been another three occasions when the team shipped eight.

Hibs 8-2 Motherwell 1893
Port Glasgow Athletic 8-1 Motherwell . 1901
Partick Thistle 8-3 Motherwell............... 1971
Aberdeen 8-0 Motherwell 1979

THE HONOURABLE CHAIRMAN

Motherwell chairman Tom Ormiston proved he had the respect of the whole community, and not just fans of the club, when he was elected to Parliament in the general election of 1931. He personally was elected with a majority of just under 800 but otherwise his Conservative Party enjoyed a landslide victory across the country.

COMING FROM BEHIND

Fighting back from two goals down to salvage a draw, or even win, is an occasion greatly cherished by supporters but Motherwell do not excel in this particular area of the game. In recent years the side have managed to claim a draw in the face of defeat – most notably at Hearts in the 2008 Scottish Cup – quite often but going the extra step to win from two goals down seems a step too far. Astonishingly, since coming from behind to beat Dunfermline Athletic in 1988, it has only happened once in over 20 years when Hibs were defeated at Fir Park. It was a relegation six-pointer in 1997 and the guests raced into an early lead. However, Weir, Arnott and Garcin turned the match around by half-time and further goals completed the win.

ON CLOUD NINE

Motherwell have only once managed to hit double figures in a competitive game, in the record victory of 12-1 against Dundee United in 1954, but they have managed to reach nine on several occasions. They are as follows:

Motherwell 9-2 Campsie 1892*
Motherwell 9-0 Queen's Park 1930
Motherwell 9-3 Dunfermline 1934
Motherwell 9-1 Albion Rovers 1937
Motherwell 9-1 Falkirk 1962

* game was replayed due to the poor state of the pitch

A REWARD DESPITE A LOSS

Even though Motherwell lost 4-2 to Hearts in the 1954 League Cup final, the players, directors and wives were all treated to a few days at the luxurious Turnberry Hotel after the contest. The club was obviously happy to spend part of the nearly £2,400 it received as a share of the gate money from the final but would have been hoping to fund a more celebratory affair. The team picked for the final had been hurt by an injury crisis and despite a battling performance and a couple of goals, it was not enough to collect their third cup in five years.

SEVEN UP!

While Motherwell frequently rattled up high scoring victories before the Second World War, since that point in history they have been a bit rarer. On ten occasions since, Motherwell have enjoyed being 'seven up' and on the winning side. It is worth noting that exactly half of the wins came in the golden era of the Ancell Babes but with the games in season 1968/69 being in the lower division and Clyde a Scottish cup tie, it is now over 50 years since Motherwell scored seven in a top level domestic game.

Motherwell 7-0 Queen of the South 1956
East Stirlingshire 3-7 Motherwell.......... 1958
Inverness Caledonian 0-7 Motherwell... 1958
Queen's Park 0-7 Motherwell................. 1958
Airdrie 2-7 Motherwell 1959
Motherwell 7-0 Albion Rovers 1968
Motherwell 7-1 Berwick Rangers 1968
Motherwell 7-1 Stenhousemuir 1969
Clydebank 1-7 Motherwell 1981
Motherwell 7-0 Clyde............................ 1990

SEVEN DOWN

There have also been occasions since the war when the team discovered what it was like on the other side of the fence. But that has happened fewer times if anyone is keeping count!

Motherwell 3-7 Hibs 1952
Hibs 7-2 Motherwell 1953
Hearts 7-1 Motherwell 1955
Hibs 7-0 Motherwell 1956
Kilmarnock 7-1 Motherwell................... 1962
Aberdeen 7-2 Motherwell 1972
Motherwell 0-7 Celtic 1982
Motherwell 1-7 Celtic 1999

RADIO GA GA

The recent collapse of the Setanta television company has left many of Scotland's top flight football clubs scrambling to fill suddenly gaping holes in their finances. The Motherwell accounts revealed the club took in £1,535,580 for broadcast rights in the season of 2007/08 with fans all over Scotland, and the world, watching various games. This was in stark contrast to the funds raised by the early days of broadcasting which saw radio contribute the sum of £23 12/6 for rights in season 1953/54.

THE WORST TRANSFER EVER?

The fickle nature of football fans can be seen in many ways. One of them is the fact that Alex McLeish is remembered with a mixture of anger and disappointment, despite leading the team to the runners-up spot in 1994/95. This was the highest finish earned by the team in the last 75 years but the general view is McLeish simply took over Tommy McLean's squad and let it decline. McLeish signed some good players on occasion but more often than not his moves in the transfer market were horrendous. Both Andy Roddie and John Hendry were unmitigated failures at costs of £150,000 and £250,000, respectively, and although Shaun McSkimming was a perfectly good servant for Motherwell, the then record fee of £350,000 represented a much better deal for Kilmarnock than the Steelmen. But, capping all of these, was the one which brought Eddie May to Fir Park. May was a competent enough player who could do a job in a pair of positions but Alex McLeish forked over cup winner Steve Kirk, young striker Paul McGrillen, plus £100,000 in cash for his services. Kirk may have been getting on in years but could have played an important role at Fir Park – a view he shared quite openly several years later at a question and answer session.

DID YOU KNOW?

Great scorer Dougie Arnott proved himself to be equally adept at pulling pints in his Wee Thackit pub in Carluke after returning. In 2009, he even returned to Fir Park to take charge of the bars within the stadium. Steve Kirk also returned to work in the hospitality department, treating guests to some of his tales about life under Tommy McLean.

FOOTBALL AND TELEVISION HAVE FORMED AN ALLIANCE THAT ALL TOO OFTEN LEAVES THE TRAVELLING FAN SHORT-CHANGED.

TRAINING UNDER DURESS

As rivals like Hamilton Academical, St. Mirren and Falkirk move into shiny new stadiums, some fans have expressed a fear Motherwell will be left behind as players will prefer to join these clubs due to the impressive new training facilities on offer. They should spare a thought for the players in 1974 as the directors noted a concern for their health as cows had a tendency to stray onto the training fields at the Cleland Estate. It was recommended that the players receive tetanus shots to protect them. It is hard to see today's molly-coddled professionals agreeing to a jab just to make it onto the practice pitch!

BOUNCING BACK

Motherwell have been relegated on only four occasions in their history, and on three of those they were promoted again at the first attempt. Much to the chagrin of other clubs, Motherwell have benefitted more than once from fortunate circumstances aiding the team's survival in the top flight. Since being first elected to the top division in Scottish football, Motherwell have only missed six seasons out of a possible 95 (not including war seasons) – a record of which the club and fans can be proud. Here is the list of promotions and relegations:

Relegation	Promotion
1952/53 – 15th of 16	1953/54 – champions of 16
1967/68 – 17th of 18	1968/69 – champions of 19
1978/79 – 10th of 10	1981/82 – champions of 14
1983/84 – 10th of 10	1984/85 – champions of 14

A SIGN OF THINGS TO COME

The visits of Rangers to Fir Park were rarely quiet. On one occasion in the 1950s the referee's report included references to bottles thrown on the pitch and on another the club received a letter from fans complaining about the use of police dogs! Things peaked in 1978 when Rangers fans invaded the pitch with the score 2-0 and Motherwell collapsed to lose 5-3 after the players returned.

GUESTS OF HONOUR

Over the years many famous, and some not so well known, teams have arrived at Fir Park from foreign shores to play friendly matches. The first was against Djurgardens IF of Stockholm in 1958, which was won 2-1, and there were several more to come. Motherwell's record in the glamour games of a different generation was sensational but it has declined in recent years with no famous wins arriving since 1989 when Real Sociedad were dismantled 4-0. While these games remain useful – most frequently as pre-season friendly games to help the players warm up for the real contests which lie ahead – there is no doubt they are less attractive to the fans who once looked forward to the rare sight of foreign opposition in the flesh. Perhaps this is another downside to the constant stream of football on television.

1958 .... Motherwell 2-1 Djurgarden (Sweden)
1959 ....Motherwell 3-0 Winterthur (Switzerland)
1960 ....Motherwell 2-1 Gothenburg (Sweden)
1960 ....Motherwell 3-2 Athletic Bilbao (Spain)
1960 .... Motherwell 9-2 Flamenco (Brazil)
1960 .... Motherwell 3-0 Bahia (Brazil)
1960 ....Motherwell 4-1 Toulouse (France)
1961 .... Motherwell 2-1 Elfsborg (Sweden)
1962 ....Motherwell 1-2 Nimes (France)
1975 ....Motherwell 3-0 Aarhus (Denmark)
1977 .... Motherwell 4-2 Ajax (Holland)
1981 ....Motherwell 5-2 San Jose Earthquakes (America)
1989 ....Motherwell 4-0 Real Sociedad (Spain)
1990 ....Motherwell 0-1 Torpedo Moscow (USSR)
1996 ....Motherwell 0-1 Porto (Portugal)
1998 ....Motherwell 1-2 Le Havre (France)
2000 ....Motherwell 0-0 Gothenburg (Sweden)
2002 ....Motherwell 1-1 Chievo Verona (Italy)

WONDER WINGER

Motherwell fans at Clydebank for a League Cup tie in 1995 enjoyed a bizarre sight. With two changes already made, a further injury meant goalkeeper Stevie Woods deputised on the right wing, a role he filled with enthusiasm.

BE ON THE LOOK OUT

The functions of the Scottish Football Association in administering the game for the clubs are many and wide ranging. However, at times the need for the body to look after its members does seem like a wearied aunt trying to protect over eager children from hurting themselves. In 1955 Motherwell received a letter from Park Gardens, then SFA headquarters, warning that a "plausible rogue" had managed to commit a felony at Cowdenbeath by posing as a footballer. The letter included a warning from the Criminal Investigation Department of Glasgow police that the villain "looks the part" and encouraged the club to remain vigilant and contact the local police immediately should the suspect turn up at Fir Park. Given the club often struggles to put a decent football team out on the pitch, the added responsibility of tracking down criminals hardly bears contemplation!

THE FAME GAME

Unlike the big city clubs, and bizarre media luvvies Partick Thistle, Motherwell have very few celebrity fans. Comedian Tam Cowan, who works for the BBC and a national newspaper, is one of the most prominent and is frequently seen at both Fir Park and away games. However, his fame is perhaps shaded by the Dalai Lama who frequently shows his support through his coloured clothes, and Harry Potter who is often seen firmly ensconced in a claret and amber scarf. It must be said that neither of the latter are quite so regular at Fir Park!

LOWER-CASE CONSERVATISM

Though the Motherwell chairman Tom Ormiston was actually elected as a Member of Parliament for the Conservative Party in 1931, the Motherwell Board had showed itself to be conservative with a small 'c'. In 1929, they discussed the possibility of placing advertising hoardings on the wall surrounding the pitch, but decided to remain true to tradition and reject the proposal. The extra money would no doubt have been handy in keeping the star players such as McFadyen, Ferrier and Stevenson away from the clutches of richer English clubs but tradition won the day instead. The club managed to raise funds at this time by going on a number of successful foreign tours to destinations such as South America and South Africa.

GONE BUT NOT FORGOTTEN: JAMIE DOLAN

One of the most popular players at Fir Park in recent years was Jamie Dolan, and his premature death from a heart attack in August 2008 caused great sorrow among the Motherwell support. The 39-year-old had been out jogging when it happened and he was scheduled to play for a Motherwell-select side in Dougie Arnott's testimonial a few weeks later. The hard-working midfielder came through the Motherwell youth set-up in the 1980s and actually played against Aberdeen at the start of the cup-winning run of 1991, although he did not feature in the latter stages of the tournament. He stayed with the club for six more years before going to Dundee United as part of a swap deal in 1997 and although he also played for Dunfermline Athletic, Livingston and Partick Thistle he is best remembered for his time at Fir Park. Jamie always gave everything for the cause and his most successful time was probably in 1994/95 when he played alongside Billy Davies and Paul Lambert in the midfield as Motherwell finished second in the league. The runners-up spot represented the club's best finish in 60 years. Goals were rare for Jamie but he did score a belter in a win at Brockville and also played a decisive role at the other end on one memorable occasion. Scott Howie had to go off injured when Motherwell were defending a lead against Celtic and despite his diminutive stature, Jamie volunteered (or given his lack of size, was perhaps bullied between the posts in the traditional manner by bigger players!) to replace him in goal. An enthusiastic performance followed, and despite Jamie conceding one goal, a dramatic last-minute winner by Ian Ross secured a famous win. While not being the silkiest player ever to grace the turf at Fir Park, Jamie epitomised the battling qualities fans want to see in their heroes. He was given a warm welcome whenever he returned for charity games and there is no doubt that Jamie is sadly missed by every Motherwell fan who was lucky enough to see him play. The 1991 cup-winning squad has suffered its fair share of bad luck with three players dying tragically young in life. Jamie, as well as Davie Cooper and Phil O'Donnell, died in his 30s and while that age is associated with footballers at the end of their careers, it must be remembered that they should have still had many happy years to enjoy with their families.

UPSET ON THE CARDS

When Motherwell's Scottish Cup third round tie at Falkirk was abandoned due to floodlight failure, the big-hearted Bairns quickly prepared vouchers to give to the fans that would permit access to the replayed tie. Unfortunately, their good spirit was not entirely replicated as many Motherwell fans chose to photocopy the hastily produced cards that ensured a substantially increased crowd at the second match which saw Motherwell progress thanks to two goals from Alex Burns.

2-0 AND WE (NEARLY) MUCKED IT UP

There are few things in football sweeter than last-gasp wins, but one of them may be last-gasp wins that come in important cup ties. Terry Butcher's side was playing well in 2005 and had confidently progressed to the semi-finals of the League Cup. Hearts were the opposition and, despite the game being played at the scarcely neutral venue of Easter Road, Motherwell seemed set for Hampden thanks to a Stephen Craigan header and a Richie Foran penalty. Even the Motherwell fans, so used to having their hopes and dreams crushed at the final hurdle, were thinking about the final when Hearts pulled one back with just five minutes remaining. David Clarkson spooned over a chance to make the tie safe, but with only seconds left on the clock, Hearts levelled to force extra time. Remarkably, Motherwell managed to regain composure for the additional 30 minutes and went close to a winner when Scott McDonald's close-range goal was ruled out for offside. There was still drama to come, though, as with the match poised for penalties at the end of extra time, McDonald sent Marc Fitzpatrick clear in the inside-left channel and he made no mistake in rifling a shot beyond Craig Gordon and into the bottom corner to send the 'Well fans into raptures. The 2005 League Cup run in full:

Round 2	Morton 0-3 Motherwell
Round 3	Inverness 1-3 Motherwell
Quarter-final	Livingston 0-5 Motherwell
Semi-final (Easter Road)	Motherwell 3-2 Hearts AET
Final (Hampden Park)	Rangers 5-1 Motherwell

NEVER SURRENDER

Having taken several attempts to bring the Scottish Cup to Fir Park, Motherwell refused to lie down in their first-ever defence of the trophy despite the side struggling badly in the league. A tricky tie at Alloa Athletic was successfully negotiated in the first round before the side were sent on the long journey north to face Aberdeen. The Dons were on top for most of the match but despite leading 3-1, 4-2 and 5-3 they failed to close out the game. A late goal gave the Steelmen hope and with the 90-minute mark fast approaching, Charlie Cox thumped home a header to keep the cup at Fir Park for at least a few more days. Sadly, the replay was not a game to remember for Motherwell who were heavily beaten while the league season did not turn out much better, ending in a first-ever relegation.

A SIGN FROM FATE

Superstitions are rife among fans and footballers alike and the Motherwell support may have suspected something special was going to happen on seeing the dates for the Scottish Cup of 1991. Back in 1952, the first time the club won the cup, the run started with matches on January 26th at Forfar Athletic, and February 23rd at Dunfermline Athletic. Exactly 39 years later Motherwell started their cup campaign in Aberdeen on January 26th and continued with a home win over Falkirk on February 23rd. Though the dates of future games in the respective runs would not match exactly, the final outcome was the same as Motherwell would lift the trophy on each occasion.

A BARGAIN AT HALF THE PRICE

Motherwell fans travelling to Romania for the Europa League tie with Steaua Bucharest were delighted to find that the price for tickets was only 10 Romanian Leu – roughly £2. While Motherwell fans had occasionally benefitted from special offers at Fir Park and other grounds giving admission for £10 or £5, it had been many years since a competitive game was priced so cheaply. Any Romanians travelling to the return leg, played at Airdrie rather than Fir Park, will have felt a little hard done by at the gate price of £15; around 73 Leu, seven times as much.

THE CHAMPIONS

Motherwell's greatest-ever triumph came in 1932 when the league championship was brought to Fir Park for the first and only time. While many of the regulars from that era are well known even to this day, there was also a support cast which played a crucial role. Only two players appeared in all 38 league games, and one of them was goalkeeper McClory. No-one should be forgotten though – even those who only contributed 90 minutes to the cause – especially as it was traditional to only award championship medals to those who played a minimum of ten games. If this was followed, it means only 12 Motherwell medals have ever been produced for the club being champions of Scotland. What we would give to see their like again, although modern squad sizes means a much larger order would be needed!

Player	Apps	Goals
Allan McClory	38	0
Ben Ellis	38	0
Alan Craig	37	1
Willie Telfer	37	0
Bobby Ferrier	36	13
Hugh Wales	36	1
Willie McFadyen	34	52
George Stevenson	34	11
Willie Dowall	32	4
John McMenemy	31	7
Johnny Murdoch	26	10
Willie Moffat	11	8
Tom Douglas	8	7
John Johnman	7	0
Tom Wylie	5	4
John Blair	4	0
James Mackrell	2	0
Sandy Hunter	1	0
Tommy McKenzie	1	0

AN EVER-GROWING GULF

The Old Firm have always dominated Scottish football in terms of the number of trophies won but for decades the other clubs, often Motherwell included, could put up a good fight against them. The ability of the Glasgow giants to fully capitalise on their marketing potential, and increase their guaranteed income each season by the need for fans to buy season tickets, has put them in a different financial league to the rest of Scottish football. Back in 1955, when the Motherwell Board decided players' wages would be set at £12 per week for the coming season, it would have been less than on offer at the Old Firm (and indeed Edinburgh clubs) but not by that much less, especially compared to modern standards. Another interesting comparison to make is with the wages in England at that time; the maximum wage that any player could officially receive was only £20 per week, so in effect Motherwell were able to offer 60 per cent of what Manchester United or Arsenal could! If only we could manage to offer current players 60 per cent of the £80,000 per week many Premiership stars earn now…

AN INTERNATIONAL GROUND

The Scottish Football Association was eager to help Motherwell develop as a club in the early days and awarded Fir Park its first, and at this point only, full international match in 1898. Wales were swept aside 5-2 by the Scots in the British Home Championship in front of what was a then record crowd of 7,000. The stadium had been upgraded especially for the occasion with clay and ash being used to expand the banks around the ground to a level capable of holding 15,000 people. Fir Park has since held several under-21 internationals and was used as a venue in the group stage of the under-16 World Cup in 1989. The young Scots caught the imagination of the public, and the games played at Fir Park attracted a higher attendance than Motherwell could usually manage!

DID YOU KNOW?

Manchester United legend Ole Gunnar Solksjaer could have been a Motherwell player. Unfortunately, he was offered shortly after Willie Falconer signed for £200,000 in 1996, so the transfer kitty was empty.

A SECOND CUP-WINNING CAPTAIN

Many fans feel differently towards those players who came through the youth ranks as to those who were bought readymade. There is a special something about watching a boy break into the first team, gradually develop, find his feet, and then become not only a man, but a leader of men, which Motherwell fans have been lucky enough to experience on a number of occasions. One of those developments was Tom Boyd, who not only became a huge footballing success but also holds the record of being Motherwell's second Scottish Cup winning captain. Boyd broke through Tommy McLean's youth system in the 1980s, and soon became a regular on the left of the defence, despite being right footed. His progress took a dramatic leap when the experienced Davie Cooper was signed and the pair became a fantastic duo on the flank with Boyd's powerful running being the perfect complement to Coop's vision and passing. He moved into the Scotland national side and won the first four of what would become 72 caps while at Fir Park. Though never one for screaming on the pitch, Boyd led his teammates with a steely determination and he showed tremendous character to fight back from injury – picked up in the semi-final win against Celtic – to play an important role in the cup winning side of 1991. That 4-3 win was the last of over 250 appearances in his Motherwell career before he moved to Celtic, via a brief stop at Chelsea, and more honours followed. Sadly, a section of the Fir Park support singled him out for hefty stick during games between the two sides but thankfully that is in the past now. At reunions and charity matches, Boyd has assumed his rightful place as one of the most respected and finest players in the history of the club.

ANOTHER MOTHERWELL FA CUP WINNER

Ex-'Well star Hugh Ferguson scored the winning goal for Cardiff in the FA Cup Final of 1927 and 38 years later in 1965 the feat would be repeated. Ian St. John, one of the most famous Ancell Babes, notched the decisive goal in Liverpool's 2-1 extra-time victory against Leeds United. Gary McAllister, another protégé of the Fir Park youth system, would also pick up the famous trophy with the Anfield club in 2001.

EUROPE HERE WE COME

In the mid-1990s, Motherwell's European experience had been limited to one away goals defeat to Polish opposition in the Cup Winners' Cup. Since then, the club have qualified for the Uefa Cup three times through league position, and once through the Fair Play League for the renamed competition in 2009, but only on one occasion were the players able to confirm it themselves rather than waiting for results elsewhere to go correctly. In April 1994, relegation-threatened Kilmarnock came to Fir Park in search of a valuable point but Tommy Coyne's late strike from a rebound off the goalkeeper was enough to give 'Well the victory which ensured passports would be needed for the next season.

ONLY THEMSELVES TO BLAME

For many years fans at Fir Park, like many other Scottish grounds, were able to change ends by walking around the terracing to stand behind whichever goal their team was attacking. The practice was put to an end with the advent of an ugly segregation fence which sliced the east terracing into two halves. This became a natural gathering point for the more boisterous elements of each set of fans at games but it was arguably the fans themselves who made such a measure necessary. After trouble flared in the 1971 Texaco Cup tie with Hearts, the SFA put pressure on the club and demanded to know what action was being taken. It took some time, but after consulting with the police over the best type of fence for the job, a disappointing solution was eventually implemented.

WHAT A BRICK

Whether fundraising schemes are innovative, or merely desperate, depends a lot on perspective. Motherwell's 'buy a brick' scheme is not especially unique in Scottish football but a few hundred fans have still paid £30 for the privilege of having their own personalised brick attached to a display near the entrance of the Davie Cooper Stand. They are ideal for a birthday or Christmas gift and have no doubt rescued many anxious children in the run up to Mother's or Father's Day. Would anyone be bold enough to give a brick on an anniversary? If you want to be divorced, email the club on buyabrick@motherwellfc.co.uk for more information.

TOMMY COYNE WAS A GREAT PLAYER FOR MOTHERWELL AND HIS GOALS IN 1994 EARNED HIM A PLACE AT THE WORLD CUP.

HOPING AGAINST HIBS

By coincidence, on two of the three occasions Motherwell qualified for European football through league placing, it was confirmed by the results of Hibs playing matches against Celtic. In both 1995 and 2008 the Easter Road men were chasing Motherwell, for second and third place, respectively, but came up just short. In the former case, Hibs had to beat Celtic at home to maintain their chances but could only draw 1-1, while in the latter a point at Parkhead would have kept them alive only to suffer a 2-0 loss.

THE BIGGEST CROWD

Motherwell have been watched by some relatively big crowds in league games around the country, but these are dwarfed compared with some of the attendances at Hampden when the club played in cup finals. Here is a list of Motherwell games with over 100,000 fans present:

1931 Scottish Cup Final.................... Celtic 2-2 Motherwell (104,863)
1933 Scottish Cup Final.................... Celtic 1-0 Motherwell (102,339)
1951 Scottish Cup Final.................... Celtic 1-0 Motherwell (131,943)
1952 Scottish Cup Final.................Motherwell 4-0 Dundee (136,274)

A special mention should also to be given to the trio of games Motherwell played against Hearts in the Scottish Cup semi-final of 1952. All were played at Hampden inside the space of a fortnight and, rounding to the nearest hundred, had attendances of 98,500, 80,000 and 60,000.

'LUC WINS CUP MEDAL AND MOTOR CAR'

A local paper in Holland was delighted with the success Luc Nijholt was having in Scotland. It reported his triumph in the 1991 Scottish Cup but also the Ian Skelly 'player ratings' in which he accumulated the most points, earning him the use of a car for a year. Luc's season was all the more remarkable considering he broke his leg at Parkhead towards the end of November 1990, but was back playing two months later. Incidentally, Luc was the first, and at this point only, player from outside the UK or Ireland to represent Motherwell in a major cup final.

'WELL WORTH SAVING

The club entering administration in 2002 prompted the fans to unite in a way which had never been seen before or since. A hastily formed working group called 'Well Worth Saving was formed with the intention of raising money to help pay the bills at Fir Park and were soon organising events which proved a hit with the fans. One of the most popular, organised by Joe Smith, took place in August of that year when 300 fans turned up at the Majestic nightclub to watch a 'Battle of the Bands' contest which was won by local group Lucid. Their triumph earned ten hours' recording time but the most important thing was the £1,000 raised towards the cause. Though the overall impact of the 'Well Worth Saving campaign was small financially, it served to galvanise the Motherwell support at the most desperate time of need.

KING OF THE WEST

The argument of who is the best player never to have been capped by Scotland is one which rages in pubs and clubs up and down the country but Motherwell fans firmly believe only one man can claim that honour – Joe Wark. Joe played at Fir Park for the better part of 20 years and made the left-back position his own. He was a consistent performer who not only excelled in his own position, but successfully deputised in goal on occasion and could even pose a threat at the other end, notching several goals including a hat-trick. Motherwell did manage a fourth-place finish, and a couple of Scottish Cup semi-finals, during Joe's time at Fir Park but he failed to collect a major honour even if he was part of two successful promotion campaigns. Though he was picked for Scottish League games, the national side eluded him. Despite this, he remains one of the most popular figures around Fir Park where a lounge in the Phil O'Donnell Stand bears his name. Joe remains the only player to have been awarded two testimonial games, against West Bromwich Albion and an Old Firm Select, and new generations of Motherwell fans continue to learn about him through the song 'Joe Wark knew my father' although the cynical may point out that very soon grandfather will have to be used instead in many cases!

DEDICATED FOLLOWERS OF FASHION

Motherwell's enjoyable run of European football between 2008 and 2009 allowed many fans to travel abroad to support the team for the first time. Naturally, as with many Scots heading out of the country for football, several chose to don kilts for the occasion. The most fashionable among the travelling army decided to have a claret and amber kilt, they would have had the choice of three official tartans, all supplied by Dalgleish Kilts. They are: Fir Park Dress, 1991 and Modern – a definite change from the more traditional colours!

SUMMER OF '91

With Motherwell enjoying success so rarely, there is a tendency to milk it for all its worth. In much the same way that Davie Cooper was honoured with a stand, a lounge, and at one point a wall, in his honour, the likes of John Hunter and George Stevenson have nothing. The cup triumph in 1991 is possibly given undue prominence merely since it happens to be the most recent. While there is nothing which openly acknowledges the title triumph of 1932, or the cup wins of the 1950s, the latest cup success cannot be missed. Clothes in the club shop frequently use '91' as a brand logo and, as written above, one of the club's tartans is named after that glorious year at Hampden. However, not everything touched with '91' turns to gold – an ambitious magazine called *'91* was launched intending to offer a "more in-depth look at things around Fir Park than any other medium" but only lasted three issues. The 50-page offering, edited by the vastly experienced Graham Barnstaple, was well worth a read but the fan base was not sufficiently large to support it and it was quietly withdrawn.

LEAP OF FAITH

Anyone curious to see Fir Park from an unusual angle was given the perfect chance in 2006 when the Anthony Nolan Trust staged a charity abseil from the South Stand. Those fans that raised enough money were allowed to put their life on a rope and jump. It says a lot for either the generosity of 'Well fans, or their appetite for danger, that the event had to restrict the number of people who could take part!

TOMMY MCLEAN – SECOND-BEST MANAGER?

Any debate held about the greatest-ever Motherwell manager is destined to be a short one. It is, surely undeniably, John 'Sailor' Hunter, the man who guided the club to the very top of Scottish football. However, the argument over who should be runner-up to the great Hunter is a much more interesting question. Bobby Ancell should be mentioned but ultimately the lack of a trophy rules him out regardless of how good the football of his Babes was. George Stevenson has a valid claim – he is, after all, the only manager to have won two major trophies – but the gap between the Old Firm and the rest was not as great in the 1950s as it would become, and he did oversee a relegation. Tommy McLean was lucky that league reconstruction saved his side in 1986, but he made the most of the break. That, combined with leading the club out of the First Division and away from financial oblivion was the first act of his reign but the second, winning the cup and finishing third in the league, was simply dazzling. McLean left Morton, who he had led to the Premier League, to rejoin a First Division Motherwell in 1984 but he made the right decision – for Motherwell, at least. Many players he signed did not work out as hoped but they were quickly moved on and others were simply strokes of genius; Bobby Russell, Davie Cooper, Luc Nijholt, Brian Martin and Tommy Coyne were all McLean signings while Tom Boyd and Phil O'Donnell burst through the youth ranks under his guidance. While the 1991 cup win will remain his crowning glory, Tommy should also be remembered just as fondly for season 1993/94. That Motherwell came up a fraction short in the title race is irrelevant, the team could outplay anyone else in the country once more and that was at a time when Rangers were spending millions of pounds on single players, while McLean himself never passed £200,000. Perhaps Motherwell and McLean were perfect for each other at the right time. There was a sad end to his Fir Park spell when he left to join Hearts in 1994, but that has long been forgotten. Some people claim that football has moved on and that McLean's style of management would no longer work but his eye for players and tactical nous would surely always keep him ahead of the game. He is now rightly remembered as a Motherwell legend.

PARTY POOPERS (1)

Schadenfreude is a word which could have been created with football fans in mind. While there is nothing which compares to the feeling of Motherwell winning, there have been times when 'getting it up' – to use the Scottish parlance – the opposition comes damn close. Motherwell have been fortunate enough to shatter both the Old Firm at crucial times and the first in recent memory was even more vital as it went a long way to saving the club as well. In 1997, Motherwell were heading for a relegation play-off with Airdrie who were not only local rivals but were a team so renowned for relishing a battle they could be heard licking their lips for weeks in advance. As things stood with just two games remaining, Motherwell trailed Hibs by three points but had to go to Ibrox to play the role of stooges as Rangers completed nine titles in a row. Or so everyone thought. A simply stunning performance, so out of character it was unbelievable, ripped Rangers apart and although the final score was 2-0, it could easily have been more. Motherwell moved ahead of Hibs on goal difference going into the last day and, courtesy of a thunderous free kick from Mitchell Van Der Gaag, collected the point needed for survival. The sense of disappointment in Airdrie was palpable and it was no surprise when they lost in the play-off to Hibs. What a shame!

PARTY POOPERS (2)

In 2005 Celtic arrived at Fir Park knowing a win on the last day would give them yet another title under Martin O'Neill. The Motherwell fans were angered before the game by what was perceived as a lack of care by the club as to who bought tickets for home stands but the hundreds, if not thousands, of Celtic fans in the East and Davie Cooper stands were in for a long day. Things were going perfectly for the visitors – who led at half-time – but when they failed to beat an inspired Gordon Marshall in the second half they began to sit back. With the last minute approaching, Scott McDonald hooked a speculative lob over his shoulder and into the top corner, and his deflected second in injury time sealed a famous victory as Celtic were robbed of the championship at Fir Park.

SCOTT MCDONALD'S GOALS LEFT CELTIC FANS HEARTBROKEN AT FIR PARK IN 2005.

THE GREATEST-EVER SIDE

Popular culture in the first decade of the millennium seems to be dominated by voting. Housemates are evicted, ice dancers reprieved and even football teams are elected. In Motherwell's case the vote took place in 2007 to decide the greatest team ever, along with a host of other awards. While this could have been a tremendous exercise, many pointed out it was made laughable by not containing any players before the Second World War. Nonetheless, those honoured were all fine servants, not to say excellent players, and deserved their recognition. However, quite what formation the eleven of Ally Maxwell, Davie Whiteford, Joe Wark, Charlie Aitken, Andy Paton, Bert McCann, John Gahagan, Willie Pettigrew, Dougie Arnott, Ian St. John and Davie Cooper could have been shoehorned into is anyone's guess! Following on from the team line-up, the award for greatest goal went to Colin O'Neill for his long-range blockbuster in the 1991 cup semi-final victory over Celtic and the cult hero was, and could only have been, the cup-winning hero himself, Steve Kirk. Preserving the post-war nature of the event, Tommy McLean and Tom Boyd of the 1991 vintage were named as best manager and captain but there would be one person who could make a fair comparison between the players of pre and post-war football and that was Dave Lindsey, who was voted Motherwell's greatest fan. The *pièce de résistance* of the night was the greatest-ever player being announced and, despite that also going post-war, this award may well have found a worthy winner. Andy Paton devoted 16 years of his professional life to Motherwell, playing over 300 league games, winning both domestic cups and playing for Scotland in the process, and was visibly touched when receiving his award from Motherwell owner John Boyle. There is no doubt that if Motherwell ever build a hall of fame, Paton will be in it and deserving of the equal status he shares with the heroes of 1932; McClory, McFayden, Ferrier, Stevenson et al.

YOUNG HEARTS RUN FREE

James McFadden may have become a Scotland legend, but he made an inauspicious start to his international career in 2002. Scotland lost to South Africa in Faddy's debut game during a Hong Kong tour but he then went on a night out and proceeded to miss the plane home.

A THIRD RELEGATION

If Motherwell fought to the last against the first relegation in 1953, and eased up towards the end of 1968, it is fair to say they never even made it into the ring, out of the pit lane or whatever metaphor you prefer, in 1979/80. The side finished last, on 17 points, and had they managed to double their total to 34 and catch Partick Thistle in the last safe spot they would still have been relegated by an appalling goal difference, thanks to a simply embarrassing goals against column and the worst attack in the league. Things started as they would continue with just one win from the first eight games. Manager Roger Hynd committed the grave act of dropping Willie Pettigrew, which served to infuriate the fans, but produced little else and the manager resigned shortly after the incident. John Hagart took over briefly until Ally McLeod, of Tartan Army fame, stepped into the job on a permanent basis. It made no difference as Motherwell's fate was sealed by the players on the park simply not being good enough. McLeod turned to youngsters who, despite trying hard, took a few beatings, notably in Greenock, Dundee and Aberdeen, before relegation was sealed at Tynecastle in the first week of April. Amazingly, the team responded to the drop by defeating Rangers in the next game but there was to be little consolation. Motherwell were still on the way down and things hit rock bottom for a few weeks more as seven games into the start of the 1979/80 First Division campaign, the side were sitting 13th out of 14 teams. And to think people today complain when not challenging for the top six in the SPL!

THE ROUTE TO MOTHERWELL

The formation of Motherwell Football Club was actually a second choice. Members of the Alpha club in the town met in May 1886 with the intention of disbanding and reforming under a new constitution, while retaining the same name. Instead, they met up with members of the Glencairn club on May 17th and decided to merge to form the club which exists to the present day as Motherwell. Despite having such a well-documented birthday, little is done to celebrate the day of Motherwell's formation. Perhaps a local holiday could be declared in North Lanarkshire?

A THIRD PROMOTION

On the idle days we all sometimes spend contemplating Motherwell's relative position in Scottish football, it's worth remembering how often clubs of a similar size are exiled from the top flight for many years. St. Johnstone, Dunfermline Athletic and Hamilton Academical have all 'enjoyed' spells in the lower leagues while both Kilmarnock and St. Mirren were stuck fighting for promotion, or often settling for mediocrity, in the First Division for many years. Motherwell have only ever endured a three-year wait for promotion but for a lot of the time between 1979 and 1982, it looked as though the promised land of the Premier Division would never be found again. However, when the magic touch was found, it was certainly something. Davie Hay was appointed after a poor League Cup campaign in 1981 but quickly managed to assemble a high-scoring side which would walk away with the First Division title and net a barnstorming 92 goals in 39 matches on the way. Wins of 6-0 and 7-1 were included en route to an easy promotion that was clinched with a fine 3-1 win over Falkirk at Brockville. A week later, the television cameras turned up at Fir Park hoping to see a feast of football that failed to materialise. A 0-0 draw with Clydebank, though dire, secured the championship and sparked wild scenes of celebration in the large crowd. There then comes one of the great 'what if's' in the history of the club. The success of Hay attracted rich suitors from abroad and he left the side after promotion and without managing a game in the Premier League. Would it have been possible for him to continue developing the team in the way he had? Or was the step up in quality always likely to prove too much for the club at a time when money was becoming desperately short? We'll never know. The reality is Motherwell survived one relegation battle but failed miserably in the next. With the club back in the First Division in 1984 it was like nothing had changed, only the financial situation had deteriorated further. The next managerial appointment would be absolutely crucial and Tommy McLean got the nod and the rest, as they say, is history. The by-product of that, though, is what was actually a glorious promotion year – for all but the few thousand who were there – is actually buried in the rancid pool of seasons that were the late 1970s to the mid-1980s. It deserves better, regardless of what immediately followed.

PUTTING UP THE BARRIER

After the high of finishing runners-up in 1994/95, a number of injuries in the following season left Motherwell in deep trouble. By the middle of January only two games had been won out of 22 and the club were on a run of eight matches without even scoring a goal. A fortuitous win, thanks to an own goal, against relegation rivals Falkirk turned the tide and though Rangers would triumph in the next game, the club was on the up. Promptly, the defence threw up the barriers and an astonishing run of seven games without conceding a goal – a new club record – brought a season-saving 19 points from 21. The run was even better considering an unofficial friendly in the middle of it brought another clean sheet! The run in full:

> Motherwell 1-0 Aberdeen
> Motherwell 1-0 Raith Rovers
> Motherwell 1-0 Falkirk
> Kilmarnock 0-1 Motherwell
> Motherwell 0-0 Celtic
> Partick Thistle 0-2 Motherwell
> Motherwell 3-0 Hibs

TOP OF THE TREE

Even in the era of players being one club men, Bobby Ferrier was something else. He signed in late 1917 and over the next 20 years would go on to make 626 appearances for Motherwell, a record which will surely never be surpassed. The next closest player, George Stevenson, trails some way behind on 573. Ferrier had a wonderful left foot that he used to devastating effect in partnership with Stevenson, and finished his career with around 300 goals and a championship winners' medal from the 1932 success.

WEIR GOING TO WIN

Suggesting lessons had not been learned from the Craig final of 1933, Motherwell often lined up with three Weirs in the team in 1960/61. Hastie was in goal, Ian at left-back and Andy left wing although Ian's quick departure meant this phenomenon did not last long.

CROSS-BORDER CLASHES

The Texaco Cup of the 1970s, and then the Anglo-Scottish Cup, gave Motherwell the chance to take on teams from England in competitive fixtures. The club's record in these competitions is as follows:

1970/71	Stoke City	1-0 (h) ... 1-2 2-2 *
1970/71	Spurs	2-3 (a) ... 3-1 .. 5-4
1971/72	Stoke City	0-1 (h) ... 1-4 .. 1-5
1972/73	Coventry City	3-3 (a) ... 1-0 .. 4-3
1972/73	Norwich City	0-2 (a) ... 3-2 .. 3-4
1973/74	Coventry City	1-0 (a) ... 3-2 .. 4-2
1973/74	Norwich City	0-2 (a) ... 0-1 .. 0-3
1975/76	Blackburn Rovers	0-0 (a) ... 2-1 .. 2-1
1975/76	Fulham	1-1 (a) ... 2-3 .. 3-4
1977/78	Notts County	1-1 (h) ... 0-1 .. 1-2

Motherwell won on penalties

CLARET AND AMBER

Any Motherwell fan playing a game of word association will answer automatically on hearing 'claret and amber' and it is fair to say that 'bears' will not be the response given. Nonetheless, when Motherwell adopted the craze of having cuddly mascots wander around the pitch before the game, and at half-time, bears were what was chosen and they were christened Claret and Amber. Quite why bears were given the nod ahead of any other animal is unknown. The exact job description of said bears is hard to fathom, but they are popular with kids although no adult has ever been known to acknowledge finding them anything more than a distraction when there is the team line up to be fretted upon!

A LONG WAIT ENDED

Motherwell fans who also follow the national team would have been delighted when striker Willie Pettigrew scored for Scotland in 1976 but they had a long wait until another 'Well player would find the net for their country. The gap was finally brought to a close when David Clarkson scored on his debut in the Czech Republic in 2008, 32 years later.

FURRY MASCOTS HAVE BECOME THE NORM AT SCOTTISH FOOTBALL GROUNDS AND FIR PARK IS NO EXCEPTION.

THE FOURTH RELEGATION

Once again, Motherwell decided that if something was to be done, it might as well be done properly. Thus, the relegation which took place in 1983/84 was utterly convincing, but utterly painful, for anyone unfortunate enough to be watching it. Jock Wallace had taken over Davie Hay's team the previous season and though survival was attained, the stylish football had vanished and Wallace's obvious, and frequently stated, affection for Rangers did not sit well with the fans. A horrific start to the league campaign brought only one win in the opening fixtures, ironically at Ibrox, and this somehow prompted the Rangers Board to hire Wallace when they sacked their manager shortly after. A change did not do much for Motherwell, though, as former hero Bobby Watson was tempted into the hotseat after a period out of the game. Whether or not anyone could have saved Motherwell that year is highly questionable as the players stumbled to defeat after defeat. The final nail in the coffin came with seven matches still remaining so Motherwell were able to look forward to the First Division for a good couple of months before moving there. There could be no complaints as the record of four wins from 36 matches was dreadful and the new broom of Tommy McLean, which would soon sweep through Fir Park, was very much needed.

A POPULAR BOOKWORM

One of the most well known faces around Fir Park is that of John Swinburne. He has performed various roles at the club, including that of commercial manager, and was handed a place on the Board in 1999 in recognition of his services. Fans will be familiar with him through his literary works that include the historic tome *A History of the Steelmen 1886-1986* and *'Well Worth The Wait*, the story of Motherwell's triumph in the Scottish Cup of 1991. Fingers crossed it is not too long until he gets to write a similar title!

THIRD TIME LUCKY

When Dougie Arnott appeared in the 1991 Scottish Cup Final, it was actually his third such event. He reached two Junior Cup finals with Motherwell Miners and Pollock, but lost each time. Thankfully, with Motherwell, he finally collected a winner's medal.

THE FOURTH PROMOTION

The relegation endured in 1984 was perhaps the most serious faced by the club. With the bank demanding money, an overdraft to be repaid, and a side on the pitch which had been relegated by some way the previous year, new manager Tommy McLean had his work cut out. Despite a derby loss to Hamilton Academical early on, the season started in very promising fashion and the team were soon challenging at the top of the table. A superb unbeaten run after Christmas put the club in a good position and a decisive 1-0 win over Clydebank, the eventually runners-up, meant Motherwell were firmly in the driving seat. The Scottish Cup also provided a source of pleasure with a run to the semi-finals, but despite a brave performance in the first game, Celtic triumphed – as they always seemed to – in the replay. The players bounced back quickly though and another good run, culminating in a goalless draw at Forfar Athletic, was enough to secure promotion. A scrappy win at Partick Thistle added the championship on top of that but McLean's job was only half done. While he had secured success on the pitch and promotion to the top flight, the bank still had to be satisfied. That happened at the very start of the next year when Gary McAllister and Ally Mauchlan were sold to Leicester City for £350,000, thus achieving the other of his goals. However, McLean's ultimate success at this point was far from guaranteed. While he had passed his short-term tests with flying colours, had the club been relegated in the first season back in the Premier League, it may have became a yo-yo side like Falkirk or, heaven forbid, have sunk into obscurity like Airdrie, Clydebank, Hamilton or Morton. The future really did hinge on the decision to expand the league from ten teams to 12 in 1986 which kept Motherwell from a swift return to the First Division. But, when good fortune was offered, it was seized. McLean turned the team, first, into a solid side in the top league, and then eventual cup winners and European qualifiers. A legacy of the 1985 promotion and – with the team presently enjoying a 25-year spell in the top flight – it is fair to say that McLean's good work in 1984/85 was one of the foundations for the successful club that now has a whole generation of fans who have never experienced First Division football. Long may it continue!

A CHALLENGING CUP

There have been variations on the Challenge Cup for several years since 1992, but the principle remains the same; the clubs in the lower divisions would play a knockout tournament among themselves without the 'big boys' dominating proceedings. Despite being ridiculed by some fans, the final usually attracts a good crowd although it has recently struggled. Motherwell have never played a game in the competition but when Falkirk were challenging the SPL's ruling that they could not be promoted in 2003, the Scottish Football League included 'club X' in the first round draw for the 2003/04 cup. Had Falkirk won their appeal to be allowed into the SPL, despite not having a compliant stadium, Motherwell would have fulfilled 'club X's' tie away to Brechin City but instead, after two tense meetings at Hampden, the Bairns were sent to Brechin, and the First Division, while Motherwell stayed in the SPL.

MOTHERWELL'S TEN PER CENT

In 2000 Motherwell announced the club had bought a ten per cent stake in Workington Reds, a club based in the north of England. The plan was that the Reds would be used to give Motherwell squad players a chance of competitive football through loans, and that youngsters in the Workington area would eventually be taken up to Motherwell. Like several of these schemes involving others clubs, it was not a great success and was eventually shelved without much fuss from anyone.